WHO MADE THE MABO MESS

WHO MADE THE MABO MESS

TIM HEWAT

Wrightbooks

Wrightbooks Pty Ltd
PO Box 2301
North Brighton
Victoria 3186

Ph: (03) 596 4262
Fax: (03) 596 4206

© Tim Hewat 1993

This book is copyright. Apart from any fair dealing for the purpose of private study, research, criticism or review as permitted under the Copyright Act, no part may be reproduced, stored in a retrieval system, or transmitted in any form by means electronic, mechanical, photocopying recording or otherwise without prior written permission. Inquiries to be made to Wrightbooks.

Cataloguing-in-publication data:

Hewat, Tim, 1928-
    Who made the Mabo mess

    ISBN 0 947351 79 5.

    [1.] Aborigines, Australian – Land tenure. 2. Torres Strait Islanders – Land tenure. 3. Land tenure – Political aspects – Australia. 4. Land use – Political aspects – Australia.
    5. Australia – Politics and government – 1990-
    6. Australia – Politics and government – 1976-1990.
    7. Australia – Politics and government – 1972-1975.
    I. Title.

333.3

Cover design by Bancroft Art & Design
Typeset by Glenvale Publications
Printed in Australia by Griffin Paperbacks

ISBN: 0 947351 79 5

Contents

1. Trying to Lead Australia Backwards   1
2. Fifteen Times Older Than Christianity   15
3. Whitlam: A Monumental Transfer   27
4. Hawke: Promises, Promises   37
5. Keating I: The Pretender   49
6. The Fable of Good Old Eddie   57
7. Power of the Secret Seven   65
8. Keating II: Making His Mabo Play   77
9. Give Us Land, Lots Of It   91
10. Investors Go On Strike   103
11. Keating III: Debate By Abuse   109
12. Keating IV: A Different Dreamtime   121
13. No Work Back O'Bourke   133

Selected Bibliography   137

Index   139

Also by Tim Hewat:

The Comet Riddle
War File
de Gaulle File
Rolling Stones File
Advertising in Australia
The Plastics Revolution
Bridge Over Troubled Waters
The Champions
The Garryowen
The Blues
Golden Fleeces – the Falkiners of Boonoke
Golden Fleeces II – the Murdoch Years at Boonoke
The Intelligent Investor's Guide to Share Buying
The Elders Explosion
The Greenhouse Effect – The Answer
A Bull's Roar
The Florey
Modern Merchants of Death
Banking on the Bendigo

Chapter One

Trying to Lead Australia Backwards

The investment boycott which paralysed development in the mining and rural industries following what became popularly known as the Mabo Judgment was NOT triggered solely by the aberrant decision of the High Court of Australia. Instead, it sprang from twenty years of deliberate brainwashing by people who should have known that the things they were saying were dangerous and would cost Australia dear.

Here are some samples from that long drip, drip, drip:

> "The Aborigines are our true link with our region. More than any foreign aid program, more than any international obligations which we meet or forfeit, more than any part we may play in any treaty or agreement or alliance, Australia's treatment of her Aboriginal people will be the thing upon which the rest of the world will judge Australia and Australians – not just now, but in the greater perspective of history...The Aborigines are a responsibility we cannot escape, cannot share, cannot shuffle off; the world will not let us forget that."
>
> – *Gough Whitlam* in the ALP policy speech at Blacktown Civic Centre, 13 November, 1972

"If there is one ambition my Government places above all others, if there is one achievement for which I hope we shall be remembered, if there is one cause for which future historians will salute us, it is this: that the Government I lead removed a stain from our national honour and brought back justice and equality to the Aboriginal people."

– **Gough Whitlam** *addressing the conference to launch the National Aboriginal Consultative Council, Canberra, February, 1973*

"Disappointment with the Australia Day statement was the final precipitating factor which led to the establishment of the 'Aboriginal Embassy', a group of tents on the lawn outside Parliament House, a symbol of the Aboriginal conviction that they were aliens in their own land. It was a dramatic and effective demonstration and attracted widespread attention to the Aboriginal cause."

– **Dr H.C. Coombs**, *when adviser to William McMahon, describing events of January 1972 when the newly-adopted black, red and yellow Aborigine flag was raised for the first time*

"We Australians have still much to do to redress the injustice and oppression that has for so long been the lot of black Australians...I promise you that this act of restitution which we perform today will not stand alone – your fight was not for yourselves alone and we are determined that Aboriginal Australians everywhere will be helped by it."

– **Dr H.C. Coombs**, *when chairman of the Council for Aboriginal Affairs, in a speech for Whitlam to deliver when giving title deeds to Gurindji people, Wattie Creek, 16 August, 1975*

"Our guilt, shame, concern or whatever, is this: that the wealth now enjoyed by so many whites has been gained by dispossession of the blacks."

– **John Stevens**, *columnist for* The Age *writing about the Bicentenary, 12 February, 1988*

"There will be a Treaty negotiated between the Aboriginal people and the Government on behalf of all the people of Australia."

– **Robert Hawke** *addressing a large gathering of Aborigines at Barunga in the Northern Territory, June, 1988*

"The racism under which Aboriginal people labour is institutionalised and systematic, and resides not just in individuals or in individual institutions but in the relationships between the various institutions...An institution, having significant dealings with Aboriginal people, which has rules, practices, habits which systematically discriminate against or in some way disadvantage Aboriginal people, is clearly engaging in institutional discrimination or racism."

– *National Report of the Royal Commission into Aboriginal Deaths in Custody, May, 1991*

"Within Australian society, racism is a crucial element of daily life, one which is deployed constantly through the media, the arms of the state administration, the practices of individuals and within the knowledge-producing institutions."

– **Professor Julie Marcus** *in the Journal for Social Justice Studies, July, 1991*

"Those who died were not victims of isolated acts of violence or brutality. Rather, they were victims of entrenched and institutionalised racism and discrimination. Their deaths were the tragic consequence of two centuries of dispossession, dispersal and appalling disadvantage."

– **Robert Tickner**, *Minister for Aboriginal and Torres Strait Island Affairs, responding to Deaths in Custody Report, 31 March, 1992*

"We took the traditional lands and smashed the traditional way of life. We brought the diseases, the alcohol. We committed the murders. We took the children from their mothers. We practised discrimination and exclusion... The past lives on in inequality, racism and injustice."

– **Paul Keating** *launching the International Year for the World's Indigenous People, Redfern, 10 December, 1992*

"Indigenous people have, since the time of European settlement, rarely had justice, and we know we will never entirely live in peace or peace of heart without a true basis of reconciliation with indigenous people."

– **Paul Keating** *speaking at a Maori welcoming ceremony at Auckland, 22 May, 1993*

The history and contemporary reality of Aboriginal Australia is a blight on our reputation, our traditions of fairness, social justice and inclusion, and our self-esteem. It is, therefore, a true Labor cause, and I call on the entire Labor movement in Australia to get behind it."

– **Paul Keating** *haranguing a conference of the NSW branch of the Australian Labor Party, Sydney, 12 June, 1993*

These attempts to fit the 98.47 per cent of Australians who are not Aborigines with a mantle of guilt for the state of the couple of hundred thousand who claim they are, succeeded all too well.

Even though more than half of today's non-Aborigine families had no connection whatsoever with this country before World War Two let alone links with the early settlers, an attitude of fault for the failures of the stone age people does grip some of the population – and not necessarily the simpler people.

Who would say that the High Court's decision in the case of *Mabo v Queensland* (3 June, 1992) was not affected in part by the atmosphere of inherited guilt which had been so painstakingly engendered? Men and women of considerable intelligence – judges of the High Court are certainly that – are not immune to current social attitudes and ambience, particularly when those attitudes are generated by articulate people enjoying positions of some power.

Even if the substance of the Mabo Judgment was psycho driven, reactions to it by Aborigines and their promoters were surely activated by exaggerated expectations, hysterical hopes.

Keating clutched it as a cure-all for the ills that he claims have been visited upon the Aborigines for centuries: *"This can and must be the first effective basis of reconciliation between Aboriginal people and non-Aboriginal Australians."*

The Aboriginal Industry* grasped it as a tool for gain. After a slow gestation – nearly a year – land-rights claims showered in: for some fifty hectares of Brisbane's central business district, for Fraser and the Stradbroke Islands off the Queensland coast, for the Sydney CBD including the Opera House, for several hundred square kilometres of the ACT including Canberra, for the Kosciusko National Park, for all the pastoral land between the Lachlan and Murrumbidgee rivers in New South Wales, for the Barmah State Forest and other red-gum areas along the Murray

---

*Aboriginal Industry: This phrase was coined by Duncan R. Bell, a senior member of the mining industry, to give a collective name to the activists, particularly those in the Aboriginal Legal Services in each State and Territory, who make a career out of advancing Aboriginal causes, often without the knowledge, agreement or support of the Aborigines directly affected.

River, and heaps more; The Wik peoples brought an action for recovery of more than a $1 billion in past profits from aluminium operations on Cape York Peninsula; the Bidjara people's representatives made a $500 million claim covering the Carnarvon Range in Queensland; it was said that some 80 per cent of Western Australia – more than a quarter of the Australian land mass – lay open to claim! And Charles Perkins, formerly the senior Aboriginal bureaucrat in Canberra, blandly declared to the listeners of the ABC's *AM* program that *"the whole of Australia is Aboriginal land."*

The heaviest blame for inflating a case concerning some tiny islands about half the area of Tullamarine Airport into a land grab covering much of mainland Australia must fall on Keating – although he protested repeatedly that most of the claims *"haven't a snowball's chance in hell of succeeding."* Les Carlyon, one of the more sophisticated observers of business life, pinned it right on him when he wrote in his *Business Review Weekly* column: *"Ah, the madness of Mabo, the cargo cult of the Great White Father in Canberra."*

The initial responses to the Mabo Judgment had been strangely quiet, perhaps because it was inordinately long and complicated – just how difficult we shall see when we reveal the true background and terms of the case later. *Business Review Weekly*, for example, made no reference to it for more than two months and when it did run a piece on 'The Implications of the Mabo Decision' said they have *"just begun to exercise the minds of lawyers as the judgment is digested."*

Certainly Canberra – particularly in the departments of Prime Minister and Cabinet and the Attorney-General – worked for four months trying to write an analysis of just what it meant for presentation to Cabinet, but very little was heard of it.

The first clear warning was given in the spring of 1992, precisely eighteen weeks after the Judgment was handed down. It came from a man better placed than most to know what he was talking about: Hugh Morgan, AO, qualified and experienced in the law and commerce, with more than twenty-five years in the business of exploring for, developing and processing mineral and petroleum resources, and managing director of Western Mining Corporation, one of Australia's top ten companies.

Morgan put it on the line at the Australian National University in Canberra – when he castigated the High Court for following "some social adventure of its own" and spelled out its offence:

> "It is no mean feat, even for a High Court, to turn the settled, established, widely-understood law on title to land in Australia into a situation where every piece of eminent, costly legal advice has a different view on what the law now is...There is the likelihood, given the contradictions built into the Mabo decision, that every new judgment will create two new problems. We call this chain-letter law."

Keating was not going to let that one pass. He declaimed to Parliament, in his usual hectoring style, that Morgan *"has never been thoughtful and he has never been a thinker. What we have here is bigotry."*

Abuse is never likely to silence Morgan. A couple of months later he was at the podium again, addressing the Council for the National Interest. His target was not, as those who mindlessly call him 'racist' might have expected, the Mabo Judgment or anything to do with land rights. Instead he was after those who the fine historian Geoffrey Blainey calls "the deep greenies."

Morgan put the proposition that for many of those for whom the god of communism had failed, the new god is the environment: *"Contemporary environmentalism is as radical an attack on the entire structure of Western society as can be imagined."*

The address was notable for the definition Morgan gave of a label he put into the language, and which has stuck: The Chattering Classes:

"Even though the chattering class is not large in comparison to the rest of the community, it is very powerful. It staffs the media, the education industry, the churches and has very great influence in our political parties, in the government bureaucracies and within industry...(And incidentally) Environmentalism is the religion only of the chattering classes and finds virtually no resonance within the general community."

(The chattering classes have come under the scrutiny of Peter Walsh, for nineteen years an outspoken Labor Senator and a long-time minister in Hawke's administrations: *"Although pre-1788 Aboriginal society was nowhere near as idyllic and serene as the chattering classes would have us believe, the culture they had may have been appropriate for that society. But today's Aboriginal children can only live in the 21st century, not in the 18th or the Dreamtime."* In a variation on that theme, Walsh gave vent to his misgivings in his farewell speech to the Senate in the autumn of 1993: *"Does anyone believe that Ben Chifley* (Labor Prime Minister 1945-49) *would have closed down mines and banned exploration in a sequence of highly-prospective mineral provinces, not for any serious environmental reason, but to appease the secular religious sanctimony of sinecured Balmain basket-weavers?"*)

Clearly the chattering classes do not confine themselves to a narrow range of issues. They are to the fore in, and warmly identify themselves with, the Aboriginal Industry – not that their friends enjoy universal approval. Arnold Franks, an elder of the Wangi people and a spokesperson for several goldfields tribes, denounces the Aboriginal Industry because it is made up of *"lefties, greenies, the Uniting Church, anthropologists and activists."*

The chattering classes naturally applaud the Mabo Judgment. And, as in most of their convictions, they are so sure of their own rightness that they feel bound to blackguard everyone who does not share it. No one more volubly than Phillip Adams, the man who made millions out of advertising, but who espouses every chattering cause, so much so that he now reads like a parody of himself:

"Our dominant culture has been frothing at the mouth about Mabo, and the strident voices on talkback radio – and the words of loathing in Letters to the Editor – have been as repulsive as anything I can recall in this country...And the usual bastards who can be relied on to throw petrol on the flames of bigotry are at it again. Those criminals with microphones, those 'populists' with political pulpits. And, almost worst of all, these rednecks in boardrooms whose only use for black is as an accounting term – as in 'in the black'.

But again the Chattering Classes are out of step with the majority of Australians. A Newspoll survey published in *The Australian* (17 June, 1993) showed that 51.7 per cent of people with a point of view opposed the High Court's decision allowing Aborigines to claim native title to land. And 57.1 per cent of those having an opinion opposed any compensation being paid if the land is mined or farmed. Two months later (4 August, 1993) after Mabo had been more widely discussed, a Saulwick poll in *The Age* showed that more than 60 per cent of people expressing an opinion recognised that the Judgment *"is likely to damage Australia's economic development."*

The investment threat is very real. First warnings were sounded at home. Les Hollings, a former editor of *The Australian*, put it in homely terms:

> "Just try getting a mortgage for your house if you don't have clear title to the building and the land. The same applies to resource projects...We are in danger of having international investors in mining shun Australia until certainty over land and mineral titles is restored. This could take years."

And the *Sunday Herald Sun* in Melbourne editorialised:

> "A threat to the economic life of Australia. Our principal export industries are at risk as miners

and farmers shrink from new investment. Foreign and local capital markets are fearful of the consequences of Mabo as land claims spring up wherever a new well or mine or building development is proposed."

An early foreign alarm came from Tsutomu Monden, chief in Australia of the giant Japanese conglomerate Mitsui which already has mining interests and is contemplating further iron ore and woodchip operations here: *"Everybody thinks we can go ahead with an investment. Then later on we might find we have to pay compensation retroactively. It gives us an uneasy feeling."*

Spokesmen for financial institutions soon followed. Paul Droop, an economist with Ernst and Young in London, said it was hard to see anyone making large investment plans in Australia: *"Mabo poses a serious threat to any potential foreign investment decisions, particularly in resources."* Mike Wills, chief broker in Australian equities at James Capel & Co. in the City of London, recalled that Australia had a reputation for allowing land rights to spoil mining opportunities, adding: *"Overseas investors would put a discount on Australian projects and stock if that situation was repeated."* Bruce Rolph, a share analyst with the Salomon Brothers investment bank in America, said that it was only a matter of time before Mabo-induced uncertainty *"could become something of a festering sore."* And Rob Davies, a mining analyst with Lehman Brothers International, called for the High Court decision to be reversed, adding with silly but telling hyperbole: *"If this decision stands, Australia could go back to be a stone age culture of 200,000 people living on witchetty grubs."*

These opinions were dismissed by Keating. He said it was *"an impertinence on their part to even venture a comment."* He was echoed, not surprisingly, by Tickner, his Minister for Aboriginal Affairs, who called them *"breathtaking in their manifest ignorance and constituted an attack on all Australians."* The *Financial Review* made editorial comment at a less-childish level:

"Mabo does have the potential to do considerable harm to investment in Australia. If there is a prolonged period of uncertainty over the ownership of valuable property rights, or if the end result is a land management regime that impedes investment, Australia will pay a high price in forgone economic growth. The advocates of Aboriginal land rights only do their cause harm by ignoring that risk.

"The government itself was obliged to concede that uncertainty was affecting investment in Australia. Frank Walker, the special Minister of State with responsibilities concerning Mabo, said:

> "We've had a number of inquiries from overseas bankers (who are) concerned about security of title relating to the Mabo case…If all these wild and extravagant and even racist claims develop overseas there is going to be a loss of investor confidence."

But the most significant cautions came at the close of the '93 financial year – from the Big Australian and from eight powerful industry groups speaking with one voice.

It was already widely believed that BHP was spending nearly half its development budget offshore because of chattering classes and bureaucratic difficulties at home. John Prescott, the chief executive, said that uncertainty of title threatened new projects, adding:

> "In most of the businesses we're in you have to secure an ongoing firm market for your output and so uncertainties, such as those associated with Mabo or other environmental pressures, are a worry."

The industry groups, led by the Australian Mining Industry Council and the Business Council of Australia and spanning the private sector, called for a campaign of consultation to tidy up problems of title, adding:

"The Mabo debate is out of hand and becoming increasingly divisive...By going it alone, the Federal Government will only end up with a position which fails to accommodate the interests of affected parties, scares off investment and exacerbates divisions within the Australian community."

Divisiveness is probably the greater danger. After twenty years of propaganda which hit a peak following the Mabo Judgment, we risk becoming set as two nations – or, given Keating's headlong rush towards republicanism – two republics!

Whitlam in his time made reference to some sort of treaty between Aborigines and non-Aboriginal Australians, and Hawke promised one. The Royal Commission's report on Aboriginal deaths in custody claimed that the way to stop *"alienation of Aboriginal people"* is to accept them as a *"distinct people."* And the chattering classes, represented on this occasion by Martin Flanagan in *The Age*, believe that *"the relationship between Aboriginal and non-Aboriginal people in this country can be viewed as a relationship between two nations."*

It should be recognised, of course, that a degree of separateness has long been established. Aboriginal councils, clans, groups, tribes, trusts – call them what you will – already control nearly one-sixth of all the land (having actually paid for very little of it) and have the right and power to deny entry to non-Aboriginals. Further, Aborigines are in receipt of more than a billion dollars a year in payouts, which are not available to other Australians, from the Commonwealth – that is from largely non-Aboriginal taxpayers.

Senator Peter Walsh – who has sympathy for those he describes as *"Aborigines and part-Aborigines who comprise the Australian underclass"* – wrote after spending time with Aborigines in the Gibson Desert early this year about the increasing number of communities opting to move out into the bush, and what follows:

> "Sooner or later the Government provides houses, sewerage, 24-hour electricity supply, an ample water supply with a million-dollar-plus tankstand, an airstrip, a store, a school, a large community hall and a swimming pool. It is a few light years removed from the 'traditional' lifestyle...
>
> "A couple of years ago, some bureaucrats I know did a back-of-an-envelope calculation and concluded that governments were spending around $50,000 per capita per year."

Now the talk is of much greater land possession and independent sovereignty. The SBS television channel, covering a meeting in March 1993 in Melbourne called *Koorie 2000*, reported:

> "For the so-called Aboriginal Provisional Government, the Koorie answer to the challenges of the next century is the creation of a sovereign state which, they say, could survive on the income from mining and tourism."

Geoffrey Blainey, as usual, sees things clearly:

> "A two-peoples policy is now at work and Mr Keating appears to be one of its strongest exponents. There is a certain amount of goodwill behind the policy but, if it goes too far, it will be self-defeating and the nation will be divided...The ever-increasing grants of land to Aborigines is probably a step towards two peoples and two nations or, worst of all, two half-nations."

Hugh Morgan detects in all this a definite and difficult dilemma for the Aborigines themselves:

> "The politics of Aboriginal separatism, the politics of black suffering and white guilt place Aborigines in the tragic role of victim-hood. As victims they cannot succeed in mainstream Australian life because, if they do, they are denying their status as victims."

Chapter Two

Fifteen Times Older Than Christianity

When considering Aborigines one is looking at a mass of small tribes or families whose originals walked this land some thirty thousand years ago – say twenty-four thousand years before the Pharoahs started building pyramids and twenty-eight thousand years before the birth of Christ.

Those originals were men and women of the Pleistocene epoch, the stone age, when the last of the ice episodes made the world a very different place. The polar ice caps were huge – Arctic ice came down as far as the Great Lakes in North America and Switzerland in Europe. This meant that the seas were much smaller; indeed a quarter of the land surface of the world was then covered by ice whereas today, because the ice melted and became ocean, only a tenth of the land is blanketed by ice. In turn, because the seas were so much shallower, many of today's separate land masses were joined up – the Americas were populated about that time by people walking dry-footed across what is now the Bering Strait from Russia to Alaska.

In the area of our concern the island continent included all of Australia, Tasmania, Papua New Guinea and a multitude of smaller islands; and the south-eastern shore of mainland Asia was much closer, embracing what is now Indonesia's Sumatra and Java and Bali. But off that

15

shore, in the Sunda Trench to the south and the Philippine Trench to the east, the waters went way down, in some places more than ten kilometres – deeper than Mount Everest is high! Further, there was a formidably deep straight separating Bali and Lombok and the other islands stretching towards Australia.

(This was more than a marine divide, although that did prevent animals like tigers from getting to Australia. The underrated naturalist Alfred Russell Wallace – joint developer with Charles Darwin of the theory of natural selection – observed that birds like woodpeckers which nested on Bali were not evident on Lombok where cockatoos and other birds associated with Australia made nests. This became known as Wallace's Line, dividing the fauna and flora of Australasia and Asia.)

Primitive people did somehow make it from Asia to the enlarged Australia. Their travels pre-dated boats; at best they clung to logs or crude rafts. At times they could island hop, seeing where they were going; at others they journeyed blind, navigating up to eighty kilometres. Clearly, because their vessels could only be small and simple, they travelled either alone or in small groups.

Geoffrey Blainey wrote in *Triumph of the Nomads* that this migration *"was one of the momentous events of world history… That series of crossings must have surpassed any previous achievement in seacraft; indeed it could have embraced the first long sea voyages in the history of man."* He has been echoed by Robert Hughes in *The Fatal Shore: "It was the first time* homo sapiens *had ever colonised by sea."*

Who were these invaders? So far the anthropologists, anatomists, linguists, archaeologists and all the other 'ists' who have worked on Aboriginal history have not been able to find out for sure. Perhaps the neatest idea – one which was accepted by the popular historian Manning Clark in the first volume of his *A History of Australia* – came from Joseph B. Birdsell, an American anthropologist who spent fourteen months in the field, just before World War Two, measuring the bones of dead Aborigines and the bodies of living ones – height both standing and sitting, breadth of nose, spread of shoulders, circumference of skull and so on. He concluded – and published in a paper *Preliminary Data on the Trihybrid Origin of Australian Aborigines* – that there had been three waves of immigrants.

The first were quite short people with broad noses, fairly light of skin and curly-haired, who had been driven down from south-east Asia by invaders; he gave them the name *Oceanic Negritos*.

The second were bigger and stronger and, because of a mass of body hair, were *"clearly related"* (according to Birdsell) to the Ainu of the northern islands of Japan who were described by Dr Peter Lawrence when he was a research anthropologist at the Australian National University as *"dirty and drunken, but intelligent."* Birdsell found a proliferation of the second wave's remains and descendants along the Murray River, so he called them *Murrayians*. It is assumed that they drove the Negritos down into Tasmania and up into rain forests in northern Queensland.

The third and last wave probably came originally from southern India or Ceylon and were thinner and taller than the earlier arrivals. They in turn drove the Murrayians southward, but did not push far themselves, staying in what is now the Northern Territory and Queensland; so Birdsell called them *Carpentarians*.

The Carpentarians, we assume, arrived not long before the polar ice melted and raised sea levels. Over time Bass Strait cut Tasmania from mainland Australia and the Coral, Arafura and Timor Seas separated off the northern islands including Papua New Guinea.

No more arrivals of any consequence were made for tens of thousands of years. Significantly, no new influences from a developing world arrived either. The early invaders remained in the stone age, missing out on evolution.

But they either brought with them or they learned for their own survival in a harsh land, several skills which people in the developing world either lost or never possessed. They could find hidden water in the middle of deserts. They lit fires without benefit of tinder box or match – and they thought nothing of burning big blocks of bush to capture a few lizards for food.

Their nomad wanderings, sometimes over great

distances, were achieved with apparent accuracy without compasses. They divided wild plants into the medicinal, the nutritious and the dangerous. And their powers of mental telepathy were astonishing.

But they had no political or social structures beyond quite small tribes, no common language, no writing; they tilled no soil, planted no crops, reared no animals; they built no permanent shelters.

Dr T.G.H. Strehlow, who was born at the Hermannsburg mission in the Northern Territory and who spent his life studying Aborigines and recording their secret rituals, wrote in his landmark tribal review *Aranda Traditions*:

> "Tradition and the tyranny of the old men in the religious and cultural sphere have effectually stifled all creative impulse. It is almost certain that native myths had ceased to be invented many centuries ago...The present-day natives are, on the whole, merely the painstaking, uninspired preservers of a great and interesting inheritance. They are in many ways, not so much a primitive, as a decadent race."

Blainey has written that *"Australia was split into hundreds of mini-republics...To see ancient Australia as an entity is to see it more through our eyes than the eyes of Aboriginals who fought one another so frequently."*

(Indeed they did. Captain Cook observed them during his first visit in 1770 as a *"timorous and inoffensive race."* But academic researchers have found evidence of horrific tribal warfare. Strehlow alone cited *"the wiping out of the Plenty River group of Udebataram from which there was only one survivor...The killing of a large camp of black men, women and children in the vicinity of Mt Eba...The grim massacre of Irbmangkara."*)

The men were not only murderous towards each other, they were cruel to their women, owning them absolutely. Robert Hughes has bluntly described the typical wife: *"She was merely a root-grubbing, shell-gathering chattel, whose social assets were wiry arms, prehensile toes and a vagina."*

Other violence was demanded by the roaming nature of their lives. Only the fit can move. A mother can carry only one child over any significant distance; so extra babies were battered. Similarly, when the old became enfeebled and unable to keep up, they were discarded.

The late Manning Clark wrote that *"the failure of the aborigines to emerge from a state of barbarism deprived them of the material resources with which to resist an invader, and left them without the physical strength to protect their culture."*

The test came with the arrival of the convict-laden first fleet in 1788. At that time, it was estimated later, the total number of Aborigines throughout Australia was about 300,000 – say an average of one to every 2,500 hectares compared with today's population average of one person to 45 hectares.

The first tribe to come under the scrutiny of the strange invaders were the Iora, fishers and hunters who roamed the shores of Botany Bay and Sydney Harbour and the land up to the Hawkesbury River. Because they never washed, Hughes tells us, they stank; because they would soon be on the move, they left their debris, including faeces, wherever it fell.

They were not attractive. But they had a defensive characteristic which served them well, as Clark wrote:

> "The aborigine was endowed with a tenacious, if not unique inability to detect meaning in any way of life other than his own; and by one of those ironies in human affairs it was this very inability to live outside the framework of his own culture that prevented invaders from using the aborigine for their own purposes."

But collisions were inevitable when cultures were so different. And the new arrivals had two things the Aborigine did not: the driving force of greed, and the instruments for its satisfaction – guns. Not that the whites always had the better of the blacks who were often more resourceful and had long memories, exacting revenge years after the event that triggered it; further, they were skilled thieves and they stole guns.

It would be silly, however, to suggest that the contests were anywhere near equal. It was, after all, modern man against stone-age man – and the majority of the modern men were felons who had been brutalised further by the sadism of penal colonies in which floggings with the cat-o-nine-tails in the 1830s in New South Wales, for example, averaged fifteen a day of 40 lashes or more.

It was in that decade that a massacre led to the first hanging of white men for killing blacks. Tribesmen had apparently been driving cattle off the squatting run of one Henry Dangar at Myall Creek, then near the far edge of settlement and west of what is now Inverell. On an afternoon in June 1838 a dozen armed stockmen – eleven of them either ticket-of-leave convicts or ex-convicts – approached an out-station hut on the property and told the shepherd, George Anderson, that they were going to muster the local aborigines, rope them together, and give them a big fright. Anderson heard some shots. Two days later the same gang piled the bodies of twenty-eight men, women and children together, covered them with wood and put a fire-stick to it. Despite protests by squatters, the culprits were rounded up by mounted police and put on trial for the murder of two of the Aborigines but found not guilty by the jury. When they were later charged with the murder of a woman and child, seven of them were found guilty. Judge William Burton ordered that...

> "Each of you be removed to a place of public execution and that you be hanged by the neck until your bodies be dead, and may the Lord have mercy on your souls."

(It is interesting, in the context of land rights, that two years earlier the same Judge Burton had found in *Rex v Jack Congo Murrell* that Aborigines were too disorganised to be considered *"free and independent tribes"* owning land!)

Henry Reynolds estimated in his *The Other Side of the Frontier* that skirmishes and massacres over the years resulted in between 2,000 and 2,500 white deaths and some 20,000 black deaths, although other historians have put Aboriginal casualties much higher.

The last recorded massacre was as late as 1928, and again there were twenty-eight victims. Freddie Brooks, a white dingo trapper with a camp at Coniston, some 220 kilometres north-west of Alice Springs, took an Aborigine's wife and, when she did not return, two Aborigines stabbed him to death. A half-caste told Mounted Constable William Murray about it. This digger from World War One believed in an eye-for-an-eye and descended with his group upon the Aborigines at Brooks' Soak and *"bin shootem whole f****** lot"*, as a witness related later in pidgin English. A commission of inquiry exonerated Murray.

It was the never-ending forays into the herds and flocks of the settlers who, in turn, were battling the unfamiliar environment to make a living, which so aggravated the whites. That most gracious of historians, Margaret Loch Kiddle – who so brilliantly covered the settlement of Victoria's Western District in *Men of Yesterday* – tallied up twenty-five incidents reported in the *Geelong Advertiser* in just two months of the autumn of 1842. In summary, they told of 3,920 sheep killed or driven away and 129 cattle taken, in addition to four shepherds murdered *"with a spear through the heart"* and another seven badly wounded.

It must be added, however, that for every black killed by a bullet in retaliation, another five or ten died of diseases brought into Australia by the whites or were destroyed by alcohol.

Additionally, as Clark wrote, infanticide was on the rise *"especially the killing of half-caste children... Sexual intercourse between aboriginal females and colonists, chiefly of the working classes, was already a great cause of misery to the Aborigines, partly from the diseases it introduced among them and partly from the hostile feeling of male blacks towards the white men who stole their women."*

Kiddle summed up the situation as far as the Western District was concerned, but she could have been writing for most of Australia:

> "As soon as the members of the Port Phillip Association set foot on the mainland (from Tasmania) the aboriginal race was doomed... Water was their first need, and very soon it became evident that there was not going to be room for both races to live side by side.

> "If the Aborigines had been great warriors like the New Zealand Maoris the result of the struggle might have been different, for then they would have won respect from the invaders and perhaps dictated their own terms. But their very weakness and comparative harmlessness were in part their undoing. Bullying of the weak is often a human propensity, and when the weak are in occupation of land coveted by the strong the issue is not long in doubt."

(It should be remembered that this has long been so. When the Huns swept out of Mongolia in the second century BC, they did not extend land rights to the Russians and northern Chinese whom they conquered; when Julius Caesar subjugated England fifty years before the birth of Christ, he allowed the Britons no land rights – nor did William the Conqueror after the Battle of Hastings in 1066, and when the Goths surged down from Scandinavia about the time of Christ's birth they denied the people of what is now eastern Germany land rights and when they pushed further south two centuries later they did the same to the Ukrainians. Blainey has put the situation, like so many others, very well:

> "What happened to the Aborigines after 1788 had probably happened a few thousand years earlier to all our ancestors...All over the world, the relatively simple way of life of hunters and gatherers was wrecked by the coming of people who domesticated plants and animals. A new economy arose and, everywhere, groups of people lost their vast sweeps of land and became

possessors, if they owned anything at all, of tiny areas of land.")

The discovery of gold in many places in the 1850s changed things profoundly. The white population multiplied more than threefold during the decade to total 1.1 million throughout the colonies by 1861; the Aborigine population had by that time been more than halved, down to perhaps 100,000. When the first fleet arrived back in 1788, blacks outnumbered whites by more than sixty to one; a century later whites outnumbered blacks by nearly thirty to one. (Today the ratio of whites to blacks is about seventy to one.)

Of more significance than the number switch was the change in position. From being almost ever-near in the early years, the Aborigines either withdrew to special areas – tribal reserves or missions or outback cattle stations, most of them in the north or arid centre – or, having become increasingly de-tribalised, they settled in shacks on the edges of towns or the inner-suburbs of capital cities. The late Professor Strehlow, an authority without peer, held the opinion that...

> "Aboriginal society was destroyed largely because the young people deliberately deserted their own people. As far as many young black people were concerned the prospect of escaping from the harsher provisions of tribal law proved virtually irresistible."

It is not a serious exaggeration to say that, as far as most urban white inhabitants were concerned, Aborigines were vanishing. What happened to them – including the cruelly-misguided practice of taking babies, particularly half-castes, away from their mothers and having them foster-parented by white families *"to give them a better chance in life"* – was out of sight and out of mind. (The author was at Geelong Grammar School during World War Two but was not taught anything about Aborigines – not one lesson, not one contact, nothing. And that was not unusual.)

Aborigines did not exist officially either; the Constitution of the Commonwealth – in Section 127 – said that in censuses of the population *"aboriginal natives shall not be counted"* and, in Section 51 (XXVI), the Parliament had the power to make laws concerning people of any race *"other than the Aboriginal race."*

There was widespread indifference towards the Aborigines. A couple of references by Donald Horne – surely a founding member of the chattering classes – in his *The Lucky Country* reflected this: *"The Aborigines are equivalent to a Red Indian problem, not a Negro problem"* and *"Asians do not worry much about the Aborigines. Their treatment of their own Aborigines is often worse than Australia's. Besides the Aborigines are 'blacks' and there is probably more prejudice against 'blacks' in Asia than in Europe or in Australia."*

The same Donald Horne went on to write with apparent approval that *"all the governments concerned with Aborigines are now committed to assimilation"* – a direction first accepted by Commonwealth and State governments in 1951 and refined in the early 1960s to read:

> "The policy of assimilation means that all Aborigines and part-Aborigines will attain the same manner of living as other Australians and live as members of a single Australian community, enjoying the same rights and privileges, accepting the same responsibilities, observing the customs and influenced by the same beliefs, hopes and loyalties as other Australians."

It was a big ask of people who had a quite different set of customs, beliefs, hopes and loyalties! But it did presage a number of changes. Craig McGregor, a critic of assimilation, was obliged to write in his *Profile of Australia* in 1966 that *"many of the laws which, under the guise of paternalism, discriminated against the Aborigines, have been reformed..."*

> "Even in the Northern Territory Aborigines can now buy liquor, own property, manage their own affairs, own firearms, have access to methylated

spirits, sleep with white women (or men), go where they like and qualify for workers' compensation and social services."

R.G. Menzies retired his second innings as Prime Minister in 1966 after nearly seventeen continuous years. His successor, Harold Holt – described by H.C. Coombs, another founding member of the chattering classes, as *"too nice a person to exercise power effectively"* – was determined to do something more for the Aborigines as an expression, as Coombs put it *"of his own generous and human spirit."*

So he introduced into Parliament the *Constitution Alterations (Aboriginals) Bill* to take the Aborigine exclusions out of Sections 51 (XXVI) and 127 of the Constitution – in other words, to admit them to citizenship. After being passed unanimously by both Houses, it went to the people as a referendum on 27 May 1967. It was accepted with 'yes' votes ranging from a high 95 per cent in Victoria to a low (but still overwhelming) 81 per cent in Western Australia. Coombs became the first chairman of the Council for Aboriginal Affairs.

All too soon afterwards, Holt took the big dive into the surf at Portsea and was never seen again – *"a devastating blow to our expectations,"* wrote Coombs. John Grey Gorton, the next Prime Minister and a World War Two fighter pilot and former orchardist, did nothing to revive them. Coombs found that Gorton's image of Australian society had no special place for Aborigines...

> "He saw no justification or need for special policies to help them and the idea that Aborigines had valid rights to land based on traditional title was to him wholly unacceptable."

So he shuffled the matter out of his own department and made W.C. "Billy" Wentworth – a great-grandson of the pioneering explorer and agitator for colonial self-government – minister in charge of Aboriginal Affairs. (It was perhaps for this work that Wentworth won Membership of the Order of Australia in the Queen's Birthday Honours of 1993.)

After almost precisely twenty-three years in power, the weary and boring Liberal government, which had fallen under the leadership of William McMahon, was slung out by the electors. Edward Gough Whitlam, the first champion of the chattering classes, became Prime Minister – and the descent to Mabo began.

Chapter Three

Whitlam: A Monumental Transfer

B.A. Santamaria, president of the Catholic-powered National Civic Council for more than thirty-five years and long-time columnist for *The Australian*, blames Whitlam for initiating what he calls *"revolutionary changes"* in our society in the early 1970s...

> "As ancient values and institutions were roughly discarded, new secular – but nevertheless quasi-religious – cults replaced them: militant feminism, environmentalism, ethnic separatism (called multi-culturalism) and insistence on Aboriginal rights."

Edward Gough Whitlam, who at fifty-six led Labor to victory in December 1972 and ended twenty-three years of unbroken conservative government in Canberra, was in marked contrast to Prime Ministers of his party who had gone before him. While the wartime leaders, John Curtin and Ben Chifley, had been of the working class, he was middle class; while they had been employees and unionists, he was a professional man, a barrister who had taken silk; while their background had been provincial, he had grown up in the national capital. Additionally, he was large physically (nearly two metres tall) with a vanity to match;

27

sharp mentally; a workaholic with an elephant's memory, and witty with it. His one concession to the plebeian was habitually to address his associates as Comrade.

He says he met discrimination (and possibly his first Aborigine) during World War Two when he was a commissioned flier in the RAAF. This Aborigine was a member of the squadron's ground staff and tried many times to join air crew, but was always knocked back – *"We were all convinced that his sole disqualification was his race,"* Whitlam wrote later.

The late Alan Reid, certainly the best political reporter ever in Canberra and one of Whitlam's several biographers, believed that he *"drew his sense of obligation to the Aborigines from his study of Australian history and his knowledge that Aborigines had been treated shamefully."*

That knowledge would have been enlarged by a case, two years before his electoral success, which was and still is highly significant in the field of Aboriginal land rights.

The Yirrkala people of the Gove Peninsula – forming the north-east tip of Arnhem Land – sought a declaration from the Supreme Court of the Northern Territory that they were entitled to occupy and enjoy their land which, they alleged, had been *"invaded"* by a mining syndicate called Nabalco (half financed by Swiss Aluminium, the biggest aluminium fabricator in Europe) to open-cut mine and refine the red pebbles of bauxite. The Yirrkala claimed that their native title had never been extinguished and that the mining leases granted to Nabalco by the Commonwealth were unlawful.

In what became *Milirrpum and others v Nabalco Pty Ltd and the Commonwealth of Australia,* Justice Richard Blackburn – the son of a Victoria Cross winner and himself a Rhodes Scholar at Oxford – heard evidence and argument for forty-four days, mainly in Darwin. He decided in a one-hundred-and-fifty-page judgment that the established principle of *terra nullius* – roughly speaking that nobody owned the land at the time of white settlement – applied. He further ruled that Aborigines holding land under traditional tenure did not have any title in law. (This position had first been spelled out in Sydney by Chief Justice Alfred Stephen in 1848 and cited down the years – indeed until the High Court's Mabo Judgment one hundred-and-forty-four years later!)

It was soon after Blackburn's judgment that Whitlam's Labor Party at its 1971 conference wrote into its Federal Policy the totally new idea that… *"Aboriginal land rights shall carry with them full rights to minerals on those lands."*

The hope of winning mineral rights as well as land rights – something no ordinary landowner or tenant enjoyed either then or now – gave a fresh lift to Aborigine aspirations. And there was much more to come.

Whitlam's policy speech at Blacktown was, as Alan Reid saw it, *"an ambitious, idealistic program…Whitlam wanted to leave behind him a worthwhile monument to the enlightened and humanitarian approach to the problems of Australia's indigenous people."* The promises were to…

- Establish for land in Federal Territories, which is reserved for Aboriginal use and benefit, a system of Aboriginal tenure based on the traditional rights of clans and other tribal groups.

- Set up an Aboriginal Land Fund to purchase or acquire land for significant continuing Aboriginal communities and to appropriate $5 million a year to this Fund for ten years.

- Enable Aboriginal communities to be incorporated for their own social and economic purposes.

- Pay all legal costs for Aborigines in all proceedings in all courts.

- Prohibit discrimination on grounds of race.

- Ratify all relevant United Nations and International Labor Organisation conventions and set up conciliation procedures to promote understanding and co-operation between Aboriginal and other Australians.

- Establish a separate Ministry for Aboriginal Affairs.

It was a huge and unprecedented bundle of goodies for such a small percentage of the population. And Whitlam wasted no time in trying to deliver. This required a unique exercise of power. It will be recalled that the election was on 2 December and, although Labor had clearly won, results in individual seats would not be finalised until about 15 December, a Friday. Therefore the Labor caucus (all the elected members of the House of Representatives and the Senate) could not be called until Monday, 18 December, to follow the Labor practice of electing the ministry, and almost immediately afterwards the Christmas break would be upon them.

So Whitlam proposed – and, with proper legal advice, Governor-General Paul Hasluck agreed – to form a government of just two ministers: himself and his deputy, Lance Barnard. Whitlam took thirteen portfolios, including Aborigines and the Arts, and allocated fourteen to Barnard.

Within a week Whitlam appointed Justice Edward Woodward – who had appeared for the Yirrkala people in the Gove Peninsula case and who later headed ASIO, the Australia Spy-Intelligence Organisation – to head a Royal Commission on land rights, including grants of titles to Aborigines.

When a full ministry was elected, the man with the best qualifications for Aboriginal Affairs was the member for Wills (later to be Bob Hawke's seat) Gordon Bryant. A former school teacher and infantry officer during World War Two, he had served seven years as president of the Aborigines' Advancement League and twelve years as the senior vice-president of the Federal Council for Aboriginal Advancement; Bryant was a cocky, cheerful character who was liked by MPs from both sides. The exception was Whitlam, who could not stand him! Whitlam wanted his protege and a member of the Queensland Council for Aboriginal Advancement, Manfred Cross, to get the portfolio, but caucus chose Bryant.

It was never going to be easy for him. For while he was

the Minister for Aboriginal Affairs, there was also a Council for Aboriginal Affairs which reported directly to Whitlam. It was chaired by that perennial adviser to governments of all colors, Dr H.C. Coombs. With him sat Barrie Dexter – a commando and then a naval officer in World War Two, a career diplomat and former ambassador, and the bureaucratic boss of Bryant's department – and Dr William Stanner, an academic anthropologist and author of *On Aboriginal Religion.*

The inevitable bust-up came over a project which, interestingly, neither Whitlam nor Coombs so much as mentioned in their later autobiographies. It involved a clash between Bryant and Dexter who, as we know, was called upon to serve two masters. It was the Turtle Farms Affair.

The previous conservative government had launched it. There was a crisis in the Torres Strait islands; the oyster beds had been fished out and there were five thousand unemployed. So a marine biologist called Dr H.R. Bustard dreamed up a plan for the islanders to breed turtles for which, he said, there was a world market. It was adopted and launched, being allocated $27,730 in 1970-71, $117,000 in 1971-72 and $250,000 for 1972-73, by which time it was under Bryant's department.

Dexter alerted Bryant that it would be necessary to budget *"for a figure in the order of a million dollars for the project for 1973-74."* Bryant said No, explaining later to the Public Accounts Committee:

> "I did not accept this advice which I regarded as manifestly wrong. If I had accepted the advice on the turtle project, a very large sum of Australian money would have been wasted...Projects on which great sums of public monies are being expended ought not, in my view, be lightly embarked upon nor, in the face of the obvious fact, doggedly persisted with."

Despite Dexter's strenuous efforts to frustrate the appointment, Bryant enlisted a mate, Senator George Georges, who was a shrewd politician with business acumen, to investigate the project; his subsequent reporting speech to the Senate would have been funny if it had not been so damning:

> "I was appalled at this massive expenditure of money. I saw Torres Strait Islanders being imposed upon in such a way that they would attract the sympathy of any reasonable person...
>
> "A company called Applied Ecology was set up and funded by the government for $457,000. Subsequently (a company called) Aboriginal and Island Products was set up to purchase turtles from the first company for $10 each. These turtles were to go to a taxidermist to be stuffed for a further $8. To make sure that there was a market for these turtles – without any reference whatsoever to the availability of a market, without any reference to whether these turtles could be exported, and without any reference to whether these turtles would be subject to sales tax – they were then to be sold or purchased by Aboriginal and Islander Marketing, which the government funded for a further $100,000 to purchase the turtles on which we had already expended $450,000."

Later in the same speech Georges sheeted home his villains:

> "The permanent head of the department, Mr Barrie Dexter, deliberately frustrated the decisions of his minister and in fact worked for, and succeeded in obtaining, his removal. I regret to say that the chairman of the Council for Aboriginal Affairs, Dr H.C. Coombs, cannot escape some of the responsibility."

Whitlam had fronted Bryant: *"I am shifting you from Aboriginal Affairs. I want your resignation." "Why?" "Oh, you run your department as your private property."* Bryant replied:

"Rubbish. You've been listening to a lot of nonsense." At first he refused to sign a letter of resignation but later, on the advice of colleagues, he agreed to go quietly for the sake of the Labor government which was in all kinds of trouble.

The turtle fiasco was scaled down. Most of the islanders remained unemployed.

Two new ministers were tried – first Senator James Cavanagh, a former trade-union hack with the most rasping voice in Parliament who was to label Aboriginal Affairs a *"disaster"* when addressing the National Press Club, and then Leslie Johnson, a jack of several trades who had at least served the Aboriginal Children's Advancement Society as president for twenty years. Through them Whitlam was able to progress some of his promises.

The main thrust was to throw money at the Aboriginal problems. Taxpayers had to dig much deeper: expenditure rose from $61.44 million in the financial year Whitlam came to power (1972-73) to $185.79 million in the year he was thrown out (1975-76) a lift of more than 200 per cent. After correcting for inflation, on Whitlam's own calculations...

> "Expenditure in (Aboriginal) housing rose by 103.7 per cent, health 234.6 per cent, education 97.1 per cent, employment 350.9 per cent and legal aid 254.6 per cent."

(Spending on the Aboriginal Legal Service came to $7.8 million during the Whitlam years when twenty-five offices throughout Australia were opened to provide free legal aid to Aborigines.)

The secondary thrust was to encourage Aborigines to become more responsible for their own affairs. To this end the National Aboriginal Consultative Committee was elected by Aborigines to advise the minister. On the eve of that election, Whitlam said in a national broadcast:

> "Our most important objective now is to restore to Aboriginals the power to make their own decisions about their way of life...We want the Committee to be a forum for the expression of

Aboriginal opinion. We want it to allow a healthy two-way communication between Aboriginals and the National Government."

Soon afterwards Cavanagh introduced the *Aboriginal Loans Commission Bill* and the *Aboriginal Land Fund Bill*, measures which when passed set up taxpayer funds to finance Aboriginal enterprises, land purchases and home and personal loans.

Justice Woodward's reports on land rights led to another measure: the *Aboriginal Land (Northern Territory) Bill*. It granted certain inalienable freehold titles and picked up two other key Woodward recommendations: 1. That *"prospecting and mineral exploitation should only be undertaken with the consent of the local Aboriginal community, unless Parliament resolved that mining was necessary in the national interest."* 2. That *"entry to Aboriginal land should be regulated by a permit system to be administered by the regional Land Councils."* Thus Aboriginals would be given the power to lock up huge tracts of land not only against mining prospectors and companies but against Australians wishing to see their country for themselves and even against bushwalkers. It passed the House of Representatives and was sent up for final approval by the Senate.

Allied legislation was the *Racial Discrimination Act*. This was not Aborigine-inspired, although it was obviously of importance to them. Instead, it sprang from the *International Convention on the Elimination of all Forms of Racial Discrimination* which had been adopted by the General Assembly of the United Nations in 1965. The Convention affirmed that...

> "Discrimination between human beings on the grounds of race, color or ethnic origin is an obstacle to friendly and peaceful relations among nations and is capable of disturbing peace and security among people and the harmony of persons living side by side even within one and the same State."

When the Whitlam government came to power seven years later the Convention had been ratified by eighty-seven countries but not by Australia! *"I was deeply concerned that Australia had failed to ratify,"* Whitlam wrote later. *"My Government determined that Australia should join the majority of the countries of the world in outlawing racial discrimination."*

The *Racial Discrimination Act* says in Section 9 (1):

> "It is unlawful for a person to do any act involving a distinction, exclusion, restriction or preference based on race, color, descent or national or ethnic origin which has the purpose or effect of nullifying or impairing the recognition, enjoyment or exercise, on an equal footing, of any human right or fundamental freedom in the political, economic, social, cultural or any other field of public life."

The method of introducing this law was novel and, in the long term, dangerous. The subject was outside the scope of our Constitution. But the Whitlam government turned to Section 51 of the Constitution which spelled out the thirty-nine fields in which the Commonwealth had the power to make laws, concentrating on the twenty-ninth: *"External affairs".* It argued that, because its Act was based on a foreign convention to which Australia subscribed, racial discrimination within Australia is a external affair!

The late Senator Ivor Greenwood – a former Liberal Attorney-General who had as much respect for the law as he had disregard for his opponents – sounded this warning:

> "The external affairs power is becoming a plenary power with virtually no limit whatsoever. It would mean that the external affairs power could be invoked to virtually ignore or repudiate the divisions of power which are contained in the Constitution."

The Opposition had the numbers in the Senate to kill the *Racial Discrimination Act* but refrained from doing so for fear of being branded pro-discrimination. Instead, it hoped that the High Court would do it for them. But when it went there seven years later the Court came down four-three in support of the external affairs power. (Greenwood's prediction was proved right, for example, when the Hawke Labor government – in its very first Bill on coming to power in 1983 – used World Heritage listing, identical powers, to overrule the Tasmanian government and forbid harnessing of the Franklin River to generate hydro-electricity.)

But time was running out for Whitlam. His government was a shambles in ways which do not concern us here. Sir John Kerr, the Governor-General whom Whitlam had appointed in the winter of 1974, was obliged to use his powers to dismiss the government after the Senate refused to vote it the money (supply) to go on functioning.

That left in limbo Whitlam's Bill concerning Aboriginal land in the Northern Territory. But the incoming Fraser government did agree to rescue it, legislating it under the new title of the *Aboriginal Land Rights (Northern Territory) Act*. In doing so, the new minister, Ian Viner, a lawyer from Western Australia, weakened but did not wipe out the Aborigines' right to veto mining and scrapped the Land Councils' power over entry permits for non-Aboriginals. Even so, when it came into operation on Australia Day 1977, as the *Year Book of Australia* recorded, the law...

> "Gave traditional Aborigines inalienable freehold title to former Aboriginal reserves and some other land amounting to approximately 19 per cent of the Northern Territory and provided a procedure for them to claim title to other areas of unalienated Crown Land."

An area six times as big as Holland, three times bigger than Ireland and nearly the size of the United Kingdom was not bad as a first grab. But there was much more to come.

Chapter Four

Hawke: Promises, Promises

Robert James Lee Hawke, the twenty-first man to become Prime Minister of Australia, massaged Aborigine expectations by making promises which he did not keep. He misled them as much as he misled the street kids when he gave the last-minute election undertaking in 1990 that there would be no child left in poverty in Australia.

When he first led Labor to power in the autumn of 1983, the climate was ready-made to win Aborigine approval.

The Fraser coalition government – having had four Ministers for Aboriginal affairs: Ian Viner, Fred Chaney, Peter Baume and Ian Wilson, but no real policy – had slashed the rate of increase in Aboriginal funding in its later years (from 13.27 per cent in 1980-81 to 5.91 per cent in 1981-82, for example).

One Fraser idea had been to purchase, through the Aboriginal Land Fund Commission, several pastoral leases in western and northern Australia on which Aborigines would raise cattle. But this blew up in his face. One of them was Noonkanbah, on the edge of the Kimberley Plateau in Western Australia, which had much mineral potential. The Aboriginal community on the station objected to any mining because the land included sacred sites. But test drilling for oil was carried out after the State government provided an armed police escort for the convoy of vehicles used by the explorers. The attendant publicity hurt both governments.

Just the same, chroniclers of Aboriginal action – like Lyndall Ryan, a teacher in the School of Social Sciences at Flinders University in Adelaide – were able to write that *"the last years of the Fraser era can now be seen as a romantic age in Aboriginal and Islander initiative."* How come? By using the tactics known as the 'politics of embarassment' they were able to put on the public agenda their demands for land rights and also for a treaty between blacks and whites, and put on the front pages critical reports by the World Congress of Indigenous People, which was held in Australia in 1980, and by a delegation from the World Council of Churches which came to investigate Aboriginal communities in 1981.

Hawke has been described by his biographers (and a great many other people) as a narcissist.* But his love of self was not enough. He needed to be loved by everyone else, too. Stan Anson tells us: *"Hawke has always been more interested in love than power."* What better, then, could he do than promise the Aborigines the two things they said they most wanted: land rights and a treaty?

To be sure – as his most sympathetic biographer, Blanche d'Alputget, has pointed out: *"Hawke, as a student at the University of Western Australia, had agitated for Aboriginal rights and throughout his presidency of the ACTU had highlighted the plight of Aborigines"* and he was *"delighted that (his son) Stephen had decided to take up the cause of Australian blacks."*

Labor policy going into the 1983 campaign carried the sweeping commitment that a Labor government would extend the provisions of the *Aboriginal Land Rights (Northern Territory) Act 1976* to all States and Territories and

---

*Narcissism: "Tendency to self-worship, excessive or erotic interest in one's own features" – *Concise Oxford Dictionary*. See Blanche d'Alpuget's *Robert J. Hawke* and Stan Anson's *Hawke...an emotional life.*

would use Commonwealth constitutional powers to make sure State governments went along with that. Formal party policy further pledged that...

> "Aboriginal and Islander people shall have the right to refuse permission for mining on their land or to impose conditions under which mining may proceed. To set aside (either) a refusal or conditions imposed will require an Act of Parliament."

When it came to handing out government portfolios, Hawke had no problem; his old friend Clyde Holding, a lawyer and former leader of the Opposition in Victoria, volunteered to be Minister for Aboriginal Affairs. He got it, but was not included in Labor's first Cabinet.

Holding immediately started work on transforming the land rights promises into realities. He arrived at five principles which he spelled out in a ministerial statement (8 December, 1983) which he called *Aboriginal Past: Australia's Future*. He said the legislation would ensure that:

- Aborigines hold land under inalienable freehold title

- Aborigines control mining on Aboriginal land

- Sacred sites are protected

- Aborigines have access to mining royalty equivalents

- Compensation for lost land is negotiated.

No sooner had he said all that than the wheels started to fall off. The manipulative Brian Burke, who had become Western Australia's first Labor premier in nine years just one month before Hawke won power, started fighting Holding for fear that land rights could deny him re-election. In Victoria, the Legislative Council (the upper house) slung out two of Labor's land rights bills. And the Northern Territory government announced that it would seek changes to its land rights act which would allow mineral exploration on land claimed by, but not yet granted to Aborigines.

The first retreat was signalled during the run-up to the federal election of December 1984. Hawke, convinced by Burke that land rights could cost him seats in the west (in the words of Ryan) *"unilaterally reversed his government's commitment to effective Aboriginal land rights – the Aboriginal right to veto exploration was to go."* This led Rob Riley, then chairman of the National Aboriginal Conference (NAC) to demand angrily:

> "If the most popular Prime Minister in the history of Australia and a Premier as popular as Brian Burke are unwilling to throw their weight behind Aborigines on this issue, then who is?"

Two months after winning the election, a cocky government – boosted, no doubt, by an Australian National Opinion Polls (ANOP) report which showed that only 18 per cent of the population were strongly in favour of land rights – circulated its *"preferred National Land Rights Model"*. This wiped out three of Holding's promised principles (although they survived, of course, and still do in the Northern Territory Act): gone was the Aborigines' right of veto on mineral exploration; gone was their access to mining royalty equivalents, and gone was any mention of compensation for lost lands. To complete Holding's discomfort, the Cabinet sub-committee on government advertising knocked back his request for funds to promote land rights.

A crumb of comfort – heavy in symbolism and very heavy in actual weight – was thrown to the Aborigines or, more accurately, to the community involved, the Mutitjulu people. They were given Ayers Rock. Freehold title in Ularu (Ayers Rock-Mount Olga) National Park was signed over in the spring of 1985 to a trust representing the traditional owners after negotiations were completed for it to be leased back to the director of the Australian National Parks and Wildlife Service. (The new owners chafed under the English name and after some eight years they moved for it to be known as the Ularu-Kata Tjuta National Park – Ularu being a major site on the rock itself and Kata Tjuta, meaning 'many heads', the local name for the Olgas; Roslyn Kelly, the minister for Environment, Sport and Territories, approved.)

Hawke won his third straight election in July 1987 and two months later started to set up his second great promise to the Aborigines: a treaty.

It was not a new idea. Back in 1979 the National Aboriginal Conference voted to open negotiations with the government, and white supporters, including the ubiquitous Dr Coombs, formed a committee to publish *Aboriginal Treaty News*. To push things along and in quest of an Aboriginal Bill of Rights embracing both sovereignty and land rights, another tented Aboriginal embassy was erected on Capital Hill.

After Fraser's then Minister for Aboriginal Affairs, Fred Chaney, announced he was prepared to discuss ideas, the NAC came up with what it called a Makarrata Report – "makarrata" being the word in the Yolgnu language for *"coming together after a long struggle."* It called for, among other things...

- Recognition of prior Aboriginal ownership of Australia

- Land rights

- Aboriginal seats at all levels of government

- Employment of a proportion of Aboriginal public servants

- Teaching of Aboriginal culture in all schools.

The government responded that it would acknowledge prior Aboriginal *occupation* but not ownership, and it would not negotiate a "treaty" because that would signify an agreement between *two* nations and we were one nation. Not all Aborigines were keen on a treaty. Pat Dodson, then of the Federation of Aboriginal Land Councils, declared that there could be no agreement between blacks and whites until the government *"comes to terms with the fact that we are a sovereign people, not a subjugated people."*

Nothing much more happened under the Fraser government or the first three-and-a-half years of the Labor government. But Hawke did move his mate Holding out of Aboriginal Affairs and replaced him with a former rival. Gerry Hand, an obscure organiser of the Socialist Left, had opposed Hawke in pre-selection for the seat of Wills in 1979 and his supporters ran a dirt campaign which Hawke labelled *"ridiculous bastardy"*; Hawke beat him by 38 votes to 29, and Hand did not get into Parliament until 1983. During a visit to Alice Springs in September 1987, Hawke made a speech in which he launched his own Makarrata idea:

> "In the longer term I hope that the government would be able to make it possible for Aboriginal and non-Aboriginal Australians to reach a proper and lasting reconciliation through a compact or treaty – I have never been hung up about the precise word we use to describe this. What is important is the process."

He added that he hoped something could be settled in the new year, the bicentennial of white settlement. But before things could be carried further, two other matters attracted attention.

The Committee to Defend Black Rights, employing again the politics of embarrassment, created such a fuss and received such media support, that the government was obliged to appoint a Royal Commission into Aboriginal Deaths in Custody. Hand named Mr Justice Muirhead, formerly of the Supreme Court of the Northern Territory, to investigate the deaths while in cells of ninety-six Aborigines and three Torres Strait Islanders between 1 January 1980 and, as it turned out, 31 May 1989; the terms of reference were later widened and the whole exercise mushroomed. Nearly two years later, when the results were released, the reports covered 12,000 pages which filled 110 volumes. The commissioners made 339 recommendations of which the government accepted all but one. The cost was $29.7 million, making it the most expensive inquiry in our history!

The latest Minister for Aboriginal Affairs, Robert Edward Tickner – the leading solicitor with the Aboriginal Legal Service in Sydney for the four years immediately before entering parliament who had been arrested during a demonstration – called the final report *"one of the most significant Australian social documents of our time."*

This view was not shared by Dr Ron Brunton, of the Department of History and Philosophy of Science and Anthropology at the University of Melbourne, who made a detailed study of it and dubbed it *"largely a waste of time and resources...Despite the disarming warnings about the dangers of ideological thinking, the National Report is itself a highly ideological document. There are a number of inexplicable silences, and many internal inconsistencies."*

At the end of 1987, Hand also announced, in his *Foundations for the Future* statement to Parliament, the scrapping of all existing bureaucracies servicing Aborigines – including the Department of Aboriginal Affairs itself – and their replacement by a body made up of an appointed full-time chief, seven part-time members elected by more than fifty Aboriginal groups and four other part-timers appointed by the minister. The purpose, spelled out by the government, was...

> "To encourage and strengthen the capacity of Aborigines to manage their own affairs, to increase their economic independence and reflect the variety of Aboriginal life styles."

After months and months of meetings with Aborigines throughout the country and as many more months of bureaucratic and political brawling in Canberra (which had one by-product in the departure of Charles Perkins, the top public servant in the Department of Aboriginal Affairs, after a row about the purchase of poker machines for the Woden Town Club for $300,000!) the new octopus was legislated into existence. This was and is the Aboriginal and Torres Strait Islander Commission (ATSIC).

But long before that result, the bicentennial year of 1988 was upon us, with Australia Day on 26 January as its centrepiece. That day some two million people round Sydney harbour watched the tall-ships' re-enactment of the first fleet's arrival. In the speeches that followed, Hawke made no mention of Aborigines; but Prince Charles – surely some sort of figurehead for the chattering classes – referred to the suffering of the Aboriginal community and his belief that its *"predicament has not yet ended."*

A handful of black demonstrators and their white supporters tried to disrupt the ceremony. But the bigger body of blacks – between fifteen and twenty thousand of them, many in traditional pipe-clay mourning – staged their own *"celebration of our survival"* well removed from the harbour.

They pursued the politics of embarrassment throughout the bicentennary, staging several protests during the autumn visit by the Queen when she opened Expo'88 in Brisbane in April and the new Parliament House in Canberra in May.

Hawke responded when he and his wife Hazel, plus Hand and his wife Maree, attended an Aboriginal gathering at Barunga in the Northern Territory in June. He was invited by the elders, as *Land Rights News* reported, *"to sit down on an Aboriginal ceremonial ground to discuss Aboriginal issues on their terms."* The result was recorded in the Barunga Statement in which Hawke affirmed, among other things, that...

- The government is committed to work for a negotiated Treaty with Aboriginal people.

- The government will provide necessary support for Aboriginal people to carry out their own consultations and negotiations; this could include the formation of a committee of senior Aborigines to oversee the process and to call an Australia-wide meeting or convention.

- The government hopes that these negotiations will lead to an agreed Treaty in the life of this Parliament (by the end of 1990).

No promise could be much firmer than that. Coombs, as expected, hailed the statement as *"a new start...the beginning of the recognition and acceptance of change in the status of Aborigines in our society."* John Howard, then leader of the opposition, said it was *"an absurd proposition for a nation to make a treaty with some of its citizens...Aborigines are Australian citizens and should be treated as such."* And his shadow minister for Aborig- inal Affairs, Chris Miles, said:

> "The government has once again raised expectations on issues such as sovereignty, compensation and land rights beyond what can reasonably be achieved."

Hawke was by then obliged to concentrate his mind on his own affairs. It resulted in his only treaty, albeit a verbal one. And he broke that.

The near-end of the bicentennial year – Friday 25 November, 1988, to be precise – saw a bizarre and unique quadrille played out at Kirribilli House, the Prime Minister's official and lovely Sydney residence beside the harbour. Hawke and his Treasurer, Paul Keating, made a pact for succession, witnessed by their 'seconds' – Sir Peter Abeles, the millionaire migrant from Budapest, for Hawke and Bill Kelty, the secretary of the ACTU from Brunswick, for Keating.

Hawke gave an undertaking that at an appropriate time after his fourth election victory in 1990 he would stand aside and make room for Keating; Keating said he would stay on as Treasurer and fight the election campaign beside Hawke. There was just one condition: if the story of this secret pact leaked, it was automatically cancelled.

Labor did, of course, win that election with a cynical campaign fashioned by Senator Graham Richardson and designed to snare greenie preferences. But Hawke decided to stay on, refusing to go of his own accord; he had to be pushed. The last year of his Prime Ministership was not much more than a battle for survival, and a losing battle at that.

There was one genuflexion to previous promises. The *Council for Aboriginal Reconciliation Act 1991* was passed unanimously. It smacked of a motherhood thing, calling in its preamble for all levels of government...

> "To address progressively Aboriginal disadvantage and aspirations in relation to land, housing, law and justice, cultural heritage, education, employment, health, infrastructure, economic development and any other relevant matters in the decade leading to the centenary of Federation, 2001."

Keating's first formal push came in June 1991, but the Labor caucus was not quite ready for him; he went down 44 votes to 66. Hawke's leadership was not safe, however; it simply went into remission.

In his final months, according to his psychoanalytic biographer Stan Anson, *"his usually reliable instinct for the mood of those around him often failed."* A fascinating moment of isolation came with an Aboriginal-cum-environment showdown in Cabinet.

It concerned a double-breasted outcrop called Coronation Hill on which BHP had spent $10 million locating and proving a lode of gold and platinum. The difficulty was that Coronation Hill is located in Stage III of the massive Kakadu National Park east of Darwin. BHP's activities had been halted there prior to the 1990 election when Cabinet decided that a powerful environment carrot was needed to secure the conservationists' votes. But after the election ruse had worked, pressure built again in favour of letting BHP get on with the job.

Then another difficulty arose: the local Aborigines – the Jawoyn – opposed mining of Coronation Hill on religious grounds. When Cabinet met to settle it once and for all, the earlier greenie values were forgotten and it was a question of god versus gold.

Hawke spoke for the Aborigines *"with passion, indeed ferocity."** Most colleagues were against him, none more strongly than Bob Collins, the larrikin Senator from the Northern Territory: *"For five-and-a-half hours we slugged it out toe-to-toe, Bob Hawke and me."* Hawke found himself appalled *"at the hypocrisy of people who claim adherence to the Christian religion – who could easily accommodate the mystery of the Holy Trinity – pouring scorn upon the beliefs of others, appalled beyond measure."* Collins: *"At the end Bob was stuffed. Three-quarters of his Cabinet lined up against him, and he just sat there silent. The seconds ticked by. Then he said: 'Maybe we should have another look at it.' That's what triggered Kim off."* Beazley, a staunch Hawke supporter, leaned across the table and pointed a finger at him: *"Listen Bob. Make a decision."* It was a call for leadership or, as Collins put it so crudely to the camera later: *"In other words, he was saying : 'Look, you gormless little shit, do something'."* Hawke responded, only just above a whisper: *"Close it down."*

That was his last exercise of power. The second time around – on Thursday 19 December 1991 – Keating deposed Hawke by 56 votes to 51. Next day Hawke performed his last duty as Prime Minister. He unveiled a copy of the Barunga Statement and a bark painting in Parliament House. Through welling tears he bade an apologetic farewell:

> "In a sense I look to you, my Aboriginal friends, asking you to say: 'Yes. You've done well.' But also, please understand, a sense of disappointment that more could not have been done."

---

* The quotations in this passage are taken from Philip Chubb's remarkable series on ABC television *Labor in Power*.

Chapter Five

Keating I : The Pretender

We have to consider two Paul Keatings; Keating the pretender, the man who came to power because his predecessor fell over; and Keating the nation's managing director who, to the immense surprise of himself and so many others, won the election of March 1993.

The foundations for both were unpromising. He entered the working world under-endowed and under-educated. His Blood – pure Irish-Catholic – came from his parents, Matt and Min. His basic rules – traditional among Australia's Irish-Catholic working class – were: go to mass, join the union, vote Labor. His home – in a semi-rural setting in Sydney's far west – was a fibro-cement bungalow of about 110 square metres for the family of six. His full-time education – at de la Salle College in Bankstown – ended before he was fifteen.

But Keating's university was what made the difference. It was an old man called Jack Lang, the 'Big Fella' of Labor politics.

John Thomas Lang was probably the most controversial member the Australian Labor Party ever had (and it expelled him for twenty-eight years, readmitting him on Keating's insistence only four years before he died). From a poor childhood – he was obliged to run the streets of

Sydney morning and evening selling newspapers, protecting his pitch with his fists – he became a successful real estate agent, moneylender, publisher and Henry Lawson's brother-in-law (his wife and Lawson's were sisters). He moved up in Labor politics from being a local councillor to Member of the New South Wales parliament to Treasurer to Premier. During his first term he introduced widows' pensions, child allowances, the forty-hour week; he launched a main-roads authority, built Sydney's underground railway and electrified suburban lines, watched over construction of and eventually opened the Harbour Bridge.

It was during his second term, at the most desperate time of the Great Depression, that he blew up a storm. He had an abiding contempt for the City of London and those he called *"the Shylocks of Threadneedle Street."* When the Bank of England pressured Australia to keep paying interest on borrowings, Lang opted for "repudiation". The Lang Plan called for: 1. No interest payments to British bondholders until things improved; 2. Interest on Australian government borrowings to be cut to 3 per cent; 3. Australia to quit the gold standard (the device by which the value of the currency was set). Canberra paid interest to London on New South Wales' behalf and then demanded reimbursement, but Lang refused. So, on Black Friday the 13th of May 1932, the State Governor, Sir Philip Game, told Lang in writing: *"I cannot retain my present Ministers in office."* Lang told reporters: *"I am sacked."* (Whitlam was dismissed in much the same fashion forty-three years later.)

Lang's biographer Bede Nairn says that his subject had *"a copious ability to hate and to envy anyone whom he thought was financially, socially or intellectually superior, especially if that individual appeared to be a rival...His searingly vicious tongue earned him a reputation as master of the invective."*

All this and much more Keating absorbed during his lunch-time tutorials in Lang's austere office at *The Century* in Sydney. He went there most Tuesdays from 1962 until he became the federal MP for Blaxland in 1969 at the age of twenty-five, and less frequently until Lang died in 1975 at ninety-eight. Lang was completely deaf and Keating wrote questions on pieces of paper. These sessions with the man he called *"the greatest living Australian"* lasted precisely one hour, starting at noon and timed by Lang's pocketwatch on the table which he snapped shut at one o'clock!

Keating obviously learned some things from experience in his time as a clerk with the Sydney County Council, with a Hong Kong trading company and with the Electricity Commission – jobs which widened his vocabulary to include terms like 'scumbag' and 'feral abacus' which he likes to hurl in Parliament – and as industrial advocate for the Municipal & Shire Council Employees' Union. But he was *"soaked in Labor history,"* as Paul Kelly has put it, by Jack Lang.

One wonders if Lang tried to instil his belief, as recorded by Manning Clark, that *"a Black, Brown and Brindle streak right through every strata of our society"* made him shiver, and the conviction that Australia should remain *"a citadel of the white peoples."* If he did, it didn't stick. But much else did, making him, as his biographer Edna Carew observed: *"A driven man, a zealot, determined to do something memorable with his life."*

Australians became familiar with Keating, the Treasurer, during the first seven years of Labor rule. There were some who saw the Hawke-Keating combination as *"one of the most formidable double acts in the history of Australian politics"*, and others who recognised him as the arrogant architect of what he called *"the recession we had to have"* – a recession worsened by his vain policies. Apart from reading that he had an interest in French clocks and classical music, we did not know if there was much more to the man.

He lifted the veil a little shortly before Christmas 1990 when he was still, we assumed, in amicable partnership with Hawke (because the Kirribilli agreement was still secret). Speaking at a dinner in Canberra he made Leadership his theme. To be sure, he could not suppress all his customary crudities:

> "Politics is about leading people. Now we've got to the stage where everyone thinks politicians

are shits and that they're not worth two bob and all the rest of it; and everyone kicks the shit out of us every time we get an increase in our salary. But politicians change the world; politics is about leadership.

"Our problem is – if you look at some of the great countries, of the great societies, like the United States – we've never had one leader like they've had. The United States has had three great leaders: Washington, Lincoln and Roosevelt; and at times in their history that leadership pushed them on to become the great country they are. We've never had one such person, not one…

"Leadership is not about being popular. It's about being right and about being strong. And it's not whether you go through some shopping centre, tripping over the TV crew's cords. It's about doing what you think the nation requires, making profound judgments about profound issues."

He was, of course, serving notice that Hawke's form of leadership was soon to be over and done with, and implying that he would make a much better leader – an opinion he had long entertained. He gave an indication, too, of what the pretendency might be about:

"You've heard me say before that when the party ended on the British Empire everybody went home. But they didn't go home from South Africa and they didn't go home from Australia. Except in South Africa there are more blacks than whites and here there are more whites than blacks. And the result was we dominated our population in this continent. So we're an accident, we're in South-East Asia. We occupy a continent and we're one nation – and we're basically a European nation, changing now to adapt to the region."

There, obliquely, but for the first time were Keating's three themes: Goodbye Queen; Racial Adjustment, and Hello Asia.

Who were his audience on that fascinating occasion? The Parliament House press gallery, gathered at the National Press Club for their annual dinner. That carried another fascination in itself. For the gallery's role throughout Labor's decade has often been questioned, although the ABC's *Labor in Power* replaced curiosity with conclusion – particularly well put by Robert Manne, the editor of *Quadrant*:

> "During these power struggles what was the Canberra press gallery doing? For almost seven years, the gallery conveyed a convincing and, as it turned out, utterly inaccurate impression of the formidable and effective Prime Minister-Treasurer *team* which was in charge of the nation's affairs. How came it that so many were misled by so few for so long about the nature of political reality?"

Yet another fascination lay in the fact that the Keating speech was meant to be absolutely off the record. Private. Secret. But when some one hundred and fifty reporters hear such a highly-newsworthy declaration there is no way it will remain confidential for long. Nothing appeared in the Saturday editions the following morning. But Richard Farmer, who did not attend the dinner, had a full account on the front page of the *Sunday Telegraph* in Sydney and the *Sunday Sun* in Melbourne.

Open hostilities broke out between Hawke and Keating and, two caucus ballots and almost exactly a year later, forty-seven-year-old Paul Keating, his wife Annita and four children moved into The Lodge.

Keating the pretender opened quietly, hesitatingly – showing none of the strong leadership he had eulogised with so much enthusiasm. But his desire for some sort of accommodation with the Aborigines began to show itself.

It had to be with Keating's approval that Robert Tickner – Minister for Aboriginal and Torres Strait Islander Affairs and also assisting the Prime Minister on Aboriginal Reconciliation – told Parliament three months into the pretendency:

> "There is a moral and political obligation on those in positions of political leadership to bring about genuine, lasting change in the lives of Aboriginal and Torres Strait Islander people."

Their response to issues raised by the report of the Royal Commission into Aboriginal Deaths in Custody was to throw money at them, as Tickner announced:

> "The total cost of this first package of additional funding measures to tackle the immediate causes of deaths in custody is $150 million over a five-year period."

It included a hefty transfusion to the manipulative Aboriginal Industry itself:

> "We will provide $50.4 million over five years through the Aboriginal and Torres Strait Islander Commission for additional support to Aboriginal Legal Services to carry out their crucial responsibilities arising from recommendations of the Royal Commission."

And Tickner threw his boss a verbal bone:

> "I also take this opportunity to pay tribute, in a very forthright way, to the role played by the Prime Minister since he assumed that high office in giving support to me in bringing forward this national response to the Royal Commission."

Keating declared himself frankly in that Year of Indigenous People speech in Redfern Park, Sydney, in December 1992. It was such an extraordinary utterance that an extensive quotation from it must be given here:

> "We non-Aboriginal Australians should perhaps remind ourselves that Australia once reached out for us. Didn't Australia provide opportunity and care for the dispossessed Irish? The poor of Britain? The refugees from war and famine and persecution in the countries of Europe and Asia?
>
> "Isn't it reasonable to say that if we can build a prosperous and remarkably-harmonious multicultural society in Australia, surely we can find just solutions to the problems which beset the first Australians – the people to whom the most injustice has been done."

Then came a passage which was startling in its depth of cringing and grovelling:

> "It begins, I think, with the act of recognition – recognition that it was we who did the dispossessing.
>
> "We took the traditional lands and smashed the traditional way of life. We brought the diseases. The alcohol. We committed the murders. We took the children from their mothers. We practised discrimination and exclusion.
>
> "It was our ignorance and our prejudice. And our failure to imagine these things being done to us...We failed to ask: How would I feel if this were done to me?"

Chapter Six

The Fable of Good Old Eddie

For the years that Keating and Hawke were playing out their charade of boon companionship, people responding to a very different agenda were putting in place a political time bomb and setting it ticking.

The way most of the media have told it, Eddie Mabo spent his time between tending his yams and spearing a few fish basking in the tropical sunshine which bathes the island of Mer, at the northern tip of the Great Barrier Reef, where he was born. All he wanted in life, they said, was to be able to call his land his own. And to show what an ol' lazybones he was, they used picture upon picture of his flashing white teeth in the middle of a broad and bearded smiling face.

Mabo was a good deal more sophisticated than that. He had quit Mer as his permanent home in the mid-1950s, sailing to Cairns in a trochus boat. Later he and his wife Boneta founded the Black Community School in Townsville, quite independent of the Queensland Department of Aboriginal and Islanders Advancement. And as an activist he had proposed that all the Torres Strait Islands come under the Commonwealth because he found the Queensland bureaucrats both condescending and arrogant. He returned to Mer from time to time and had built

57

a typical holiday house for his family beside a lovely beach not far from the main village of Las.

Mabo was a striking figure at a conference on Race Relations and Land Rights held at James Cook University in Townsville in 1981. Luminaries of the chattering classes in attendance included Dr Coombs, inevitably; Garth Nettheim, long-time professor of law at the University of New South Wales and author of books on Aborigines and the law, and Al Grasby, whom Whitlam had earlier appointed the first Commissioner for Community Relations after losing his parliamentary seat of Riverina.

Greg McIntyre, a solicitor who had been involved in land rights since his early days in Perth and who was then practising in Cairns, presented a paper which canvassed ways of overthrowing the principle of *terra nullius* on which *"the white Australian nation is founded."*

This paper attracted the attention of Mabo and his mate from Mer, the Anglican vicar David Passi, and of two visitors from Melbourne, the barrister Barbara Hocking and the anthropologist Dr Nonie Sharp, who teaches in the Department of Sociology at LaTrobe University and who first visited Mer in 1978.

They converged on McIntyre and, after informal discussion, it was resolved to mount a challenge to Blackburn's judgment in the Yirrkala case on the Gove Peninsula in 1971 *(covered in Chapter Three)* by taking the Mer islanders' claims to the High Court *"on the basis of customary land law."*

It was actually good thinking. For the people of what are known to whites as the Murray Islands – the volcanic Mer, by far the biggest but still only a few square kilometres, and its two tiny companions-in-coral Dauar and Waier – are former Melanesian headhunters with settled habits; they have very little in common with mainland Aborigines. The Meriams, despite a ferocious past, are into such peaceful pursuits as gardening and fishing – each family's land has long been marked out and handed down from generation to generation.

The Meriams also have a religious structure, given to them by the god Malo who arrived in the form of an octopus, his tentacles representing the eight clans on the islands whom he unified. He is said to have taught them how to slaughter their enemies – and here there is some doubt as to how much is true verbal history and how much stems from the bloody bestseller *Drums of Mer,* written in 1933 by Ion L. Idriess, the prolific author of faction who claimed : *"This story is in all essentials historical fact."* Malo also taught them how to grow things and look after the land.

White contacts were few: sailing ships sheltering; the explorer Matthew Flinders called in on *Investigator* in 1802 and noted *"Indians of dark-chocolate – active, muscular men";* two British castaways succoured for two years in the 1830s until they were picked up by a passing vessel. Missionaries arrived on Mer in 1871 in what is recounted as *"the coming of the light"* and, because the islanders saw a connection between their teachings and those of Malo, made many converts; the Rev. Passi maintains that Malo was not destroyed by the missionaries because *"Malo came to prepare the world for a bigger truth: Jesus Christ is where Malo was pointing."*

Queensland formally annexed all the Torres Strait islands in 1879; the Mabo plaintiffs later called it *"a naval act of war"* because Captain Pennefather in *HMS Pearl* fired some shots over Warrior Island, 100 kilometres west of Mer, as a warning to the inhabitants not to repeat the folly of their forebears who had sought battle with Bligh, of *Bounty* fame, some eighty-seven years earlier!

The decision of the gathering at James Cook University to mount a challenge based on Mer was shrewd, and a good campaign-in-progress account by Nonie Sharp was published in *Arena,* the quarterly "Marxist Journal of Criticism and Discussion" in 1991.

(It is interesting that some sixty years ago the Communist Party of Australia included in its program: *"The handing over to the Aborigines of large tracts of watered and fertile country, with towns, sea ports, railways, roads, etc., to become one or more independent Aboriginal states or republics."*)

The strategists organised five Meriams to make direct application in May 1982 to the High Court – as the

Constitution allows under particular circumstances – for relief from a threat by the Queensland government to introduce deeds of grant over property on Mer which would have upset all traditional arrangements, and laying claim to land and adjacent reefs. The plaintiffs were: Eddie Koiki Mabo, Celuia Salee (who has since died), the Rev. Dave Passi, Sam Passi (who later withdrew after some disagreement) and James Rice, who was then chairman of the local council.

The claims were importantly different to those made by the Yirrkala people on Gove: where the Yirrkala had claimed *communal* title to the land, the Meriams laid *individual* claims to specific blocks in both villages and gardens.

As Sharp reported: *"The years following 1982 saw an evolving drama, with plots and sub-plots and the odd counter plot."*

The Queensland government of Johannes Bjelke-Petersen, then in his seventy-fifth year and seventeenth year as Premier, tried to halt the Mabo case in its tracks by passing just before Easter 1985 the *Queensland Coast Islands Declaratory Act* which wiped out retrospectively any and all land rights on Mer which survived the annexation of 1879.

The Meriams' legal team – led by Aaron Ronald Castan, a sound Melbourne QC then aged forty-five, with Barbara Hocking and Bryan Keon-Cohen (who taught law at Monash University and had written in favour of Aboriginal self-government) briefed by Greg McIntyre – fired in an objection on their behalf which claimed that Queensland had no proper power to take away their rights retrospectively.

Now, the High Court is a court which listens to learned argument rather than evidence; its job, under Section 73 of the Constitution, is to hear and determine cases *"as to questions of law only."* So, before hearing arguments on the Miriams' legal demurrer (objection), it sent the case to Judge Martin Moynihan, of the Supreme Court of Queensland, to listen to the evidence and reach conclusions on the facts of the matter.

The legal system in Australia is notoriously (some

The Fable of Good Old Eddie

would say scandalously) slow, and it was October 1986 before Moynihan started listening to witnesses in Brisbane. The first was Eddie Mabo, and the judge heard him for days.

During Mabo's evidence the State of Queensland raised 289 objections. Why? Because the practice on Mer was and is to transfer land orally – *"I give you, my son Jakara, the yam garden. And I leave you, my son Beizam, the banana plantation."* But under Australia's common law system this is hearsay evidence and is, therefore, inadmissible.

Verbal testimony has another difficulty. It is often wrong! Dr Ron Brunton has studied the data on this and, in his paper *Mabo and Oral Traditions*, finds:

> "There is an unfortunate tendency amongst Westerners to assume that the memories of people in tribal societies are far more reliable than those of people in our own society, and such beliefs gain credibility from accounts of non-literate performers who can recite extremely long epics or songs without faltering. But this does not mean that the content will be repeated without variation from performance to performance."

And this:

> "There is widespread acknowledgement of the malleability of tribal cultures and societies, and a recognition of the ease with which changes can be forgotten or disguised, usually with complete sincerity."

Brunton goes on to point out that indigenous people have long absorbed information from outsiders and included it in their 'traditional' histories. He cites Aboriginal stories about...

> "Captain Cook visiting places great distances from his actual landings, including the Kimberley region of Western Australia. In one story

from the Victoria River district of the Northern Territory, Ned Kelly was the first European to make contact with the Aborigines, and he was followed by Captain Cook, who shot him."

Judge Moynihan became well aware of this and of the fact that Mabo had read Idriess' *Drums of Mer* as well as the *Reports of the Cambridge Anthropological Expedition to Torres Strait*, also prepared in the 1930s. He wrote: *"I am inclined to think his accounts...owe more to those books than they do to any oral history."* The judge doubted other things about Mabo's evidence, too:

> "In my view (he) is quite capable of tailoring his story to whatever shape he perceives would advance his cause...I would not be inclined to act on his evidence in a matter bearing on his self-interest (and most of his evidence was of this character one way or another) unless it was corroborated."

Before Judge Moynihan gave his ruling on the admissibility of oral evidence, the scene switched to Canberra. The High Court heard submissions on Queensland's *Coast Islands Declaratory Act* in March of 1988 and gave its ruling nine months later. (This was the judgment in Mabo v Queensland (No.1), not to be confused with *No.2* which came four years later and is generally known as the Mabo Judgment.)

In a split four-three decision it said that the Act violated Section 10(1) of the *Racial Discrimination Act 1975* which enforces equality under both Commonwealth and State laws. The crucial point – as Tony Blackshield, Professor of Law at Macquarie University, has made clear – is that the Queensland Act was *inconsistent* with the Commonwealth Act and that offended Section 109 of the Constitution, which says:

> "When a law of a State is inconsistent with a law of the Commonwealth, the latter shall prevail,

and the former shall, to the extent of the inconsistency, be invalid."

(This vital factor was not grasped by several Premiers and others who, following *No.2* and the elevation of the whole Mabo debate, talked blithely about solving the problems via State legislation – as we shall see.)

The majority in *No.1* added another dimension when it recognised for the first time a system of owning and inheriting land which was different to the established law of title in Australia. In effect, they hit on the head objections to verbal transfer of title as practised on Mer.

As a result, when Moynihan resumed hearing evidence on Mer in mid-1989, counsel for Queensland abondoned objections against hearsay evidence. The angle of attack was switched to the point made by Patrick Killoran, for more than twenty-five years a senior officer in the Department of Community Services, who claimed in an affidavit rebutting the original islanders' claims that *"the former modes of life of the Murray Islanders"* had been fundamentally altered by outsiders. But the plaintiffs testified strongly that, although there had certainly been changes, they lived by the traditions of Mer and Malo's law which had been taught to them by their grandfathers.

Judge Moynihan acknowledged *"the difficulty of speaking of the concepts of one culture from the perspective of another"* but, after hearing evidence for sixty-six days, he determined, near the close of 1990, that:

> "I have little difficulty in accepting that the people of the Murray Islands perceive themselves as having an enduring relationship with land on the islands and the seas and reefs surrounding them."

The case passed back to the High Court for argument and decision. But six months before the judgment was handed down, the mainplayer died. Eddie Mabo succumbed to cancer in January 1992, aged fifty-five – not knowing whether he had won or lost.

Chapter Seven

Power of the Secret Seven

For an institution of such importance and so much power, the High Court of Australia is guilty of hiding its light under a bushel; it is in urgent need of a good public relations consultant. Not one citizen in a hundred could tell you the name of just one of its Justices, let alone the seven; and one suspects that most law students would be hard pressed to identify more than two or three.

When a good percentage of Australians are familiar with and have a view about Prime Ministers and Premiers and both Federal and State ministers, it is surely strange and bordering on a scandal that the handful of people who can throw into question ownership of vast tracts of our land, as they have with their Mabo Judgment, form what is virtually a secret society.

The High Court was born of Federation and, since appeals to the Queen's Privy Council in London were finally abolished by proclamation of the *Australia Act* in 1986, is indisputably the most powerful court in the land – more powerful in some regards, as we shall see, than the democratically-elected Parliament.

From the beginning it was seen by the writers of the Constitution, who chose to follow the American pattern, as the third side of the ruling Commonwealth triangle, the other two being the executive – the government of the day

– and the Parliament. Alfred Deakin called it, when introducing the Bill to establish the Court in 1903, *"the keystone of the Federal arch, the competent tribunal to protect the Constitution (and able to decide) the orbit and boundary of every power."*

Originally there were just three judges: Chief Justice Sir Samuel Griffith, former Premier and Chief Justice of Queensland whom Manning Clark characterised as *"champion of the Bar and champion of that other bar which Australians accept as the criterion of a man's worth"*; Justice Sir Edmund Barton, who had served as the first Prime Minister of Australia but who was similarly known to his friends and enemies as *"toss-pot Barton"*, and Justice Richard Edward O'Connor, former solicitor-general of New South Wales and long-time crony of Barton's. This trio, who had all run strenuous political races in their time, might have looked upon the Court as semi-retirement; if so they were extraordinarily well rewarded: the Chief received £3,500 a year (which translates to $333,000 at 1993 values) and the Justices £3,000 ($285,000).

The brotherhood was enlarged to five judges in 1906 and to seven in 1912. It remains at seven, although one of their number today is a sister! In June 1992, when the main Mabo Judgment – *Mabo No. 2* – was delivered, members of the Court were, in order of seniority:

- **Chief Justice Anthony Frank Mason**, then aged 67, who was appointed to the Court by the McMahon coalition government in August 1972 and who was made Chief by the Hawke Labor government in 1987. He grew up in Sydney, became a Flying Officer in the RAAF towards the end of World War Two, did arts and law at the University of Sydney, was admitted to the New South Wales Bar in 1951 and became a QC in 1964. He was Commonwealth Solicitor-General for five years and sat as a judge in the Court of Appeal of the Supreme Court of New South Wales for three years. His salary at the time of Mabo was $185,251 (now $191,550), so the remuneration has slipped back over the ninety years!

Power of the Secret Seven

- **Justice Francis Gerard Brennan**, then 64, was appointed by the Fraser coalition government in February 1981. The son of a judge, he grew up in Rockhampton and Toowoomba. He became president of the National Union of Students while doing arts and law at the University of Queensland. Later he was president of the Bar Association of Queensland for three years and also of the Australian Bar Asociation. He was made the first president of the Administrative Appeals Tribunal in 1976 and a judge of the Federal Court and of the Supreme Court of the ACT. In common with the other Justices of the Court his salary was $168,397 (now $174,122) so they, too, are not as well paid as the first Justices.

- **Justice William Patrick Deane**, then 61, appointed by the Fraser government in July 1982. Another Sydneysider, he graduated in arts and law and then did additional studies at Trinity College in Dublin and at The Hague. Before his appointment, he had been, in turn, a judge of the Supreme Court of New South Wales, a judge of the Federal Court and president of the Trade Practices Tribunal.

- **Justice Daryl Michael Dawson**, then 59, was appointed by the Fraser government in August 1982. He took honours in law at the University of Melbourne and went to the United States on a Fulbright Scholarship and took his master's degree in law at Yale. He became a Lieutenant-Commander in the RANVR. For the eight years prior to his appointment he was Solicitor-General of Victoria.

- **Justice John Leslie Toohey**, then 62, was appointed by the Hawke government in February 1987. Only the second Western Australian to join the Court since World War Two, he had considerable experience in the Mabo area. He had been part of the Aboriginal Legal Service of North-West Australia and for five years served as Aboriginal Land Commissioner in the Northern Territory.

- **Justice Mary Genevieve Gaudron**, then 49, the first woman appointed to the Court, by the Hawke government in February 1987. She had also been the first woman member of the Bar Council of New South Wales and the first female deputy-president of the Australian Conciliation and Arbitration Commission. At the time of her appointment she was Solicitor-General of New South Wales. Bob Hawke has said of her: *"She is an extraordinarily intelligent woman, but she has an unnerving manner: she giggles."*

- **Justice Michael Hudson McHugh**, then 56, was appointed by the Hawke government in February 1989, the fourth of the seven to belong to the New South Wales Bar and the only one with a strong enthusiasm for horse-racing. Prior to joining the Court he was a judge of the New South Wales Court of Appeal.

The four appointed by Conservative governments – Mason, Brennan, Deane and Dawson – were knighted. All six men were made Companions in the General Division of the Order of Australia by the Hawke government – this was not gender preferment; Gaudron declined it.

The Justices work in one of the most striking buildings in Canberra, a spectacular (but not to all eyes pleasing) pile of 18,400 cubic metres of bush-hammered concrete and some 4,000 square metres of glass. It is set beside Lake Burley Griffin, next to the National Gallery and near the National Library. It was opened by the Queen in May 1980.

It is not just the building which has a modern style. The Court itself has changed profoundly, some would say too profoundly.

For the first thirty years after World War Two the Court saw its role as that of the strictly-legal interpreter of the Constitution and of the common law. Sir Owen Dixon – who sat on the High Court bench for an incredible thirty-five years and who R.G. Menzies described as *"the greatest lawyer in Australian legal history"* – spelled it out when he was sworn in as the Chief Justice in 1952:

"The Court's sole function is to interpret a constitutional description of power or restraint upon power and say whether a given measure falls on one side of a line consequently drawn or on the other, and that it has nothing whatever to do with the merits or demerits of the measure...It may be that the Court is thought to be excessively legalistic. I should be sorry to think that it is anything else. There is no other guide to judicial decision in great conflicts than a strict and complete legalism."

(Menzies, a top barrister in his own right, believed: *"The High Court is a court of law and not one of sociological opinion."*)

Consider now the words of Dixon's successor three times removed, nearly thirty years on – today's Sir Anthony Mason:

"Legalism is unachievable and so illusory; it conceals the true basis of decision-making. Values are important to legal reasoning; the values should be stated explicitly; they should be current community values. A Constitution above all cannot be interpreted legalistically."

So where does this judicial switch leave us?

Brian Galligan, Professor of Political Science at the Australian National University, author of *Politics of the High Court* and firm believer that the modern High Court *MAKES* the Constitution and *MAKES* the common law, gives one answer:

"The change from legalism to realism is not simply one of public rhetoric...The Court is now self-consciously developing the Constitution to suit the needs of the Australian people in modern times; and changing laws, as in Mabo, to reflect community and international standards on rights... Judges are looking more to considerations of national purpose, to policy consequences, to historical context, and to internat- ional accords."

Another answer comes from that bright broth of a boyo Padraic P. McGuinness in his column in *The Australian*:

"It needs to be recognised that in our legal system the common law is what the High Court says it is, however tortuous the arguments it uses to pretend it is building on tradition."

And a third comes from Michael Lavarch, the young Attorney-General in the Keating government:

"The High Court has always made law. Mabo is a common law decision – and common law is JUDGE-MADE LAW."

Which brings us to *Mabo No.2 – Mabo and Others v State of Queensland* and the various judgments which the full bench handed down ten years after the legal saga was launched formally. They filled more than two hundred packed pages and, to the layman, were of mind-numbing obscurity. The six-one majority in favour of the islanders' land rights was cobbled up on what the Chief Justice later called a technicality...

"We had six judges who were in favour of Aboriginal land rights on a common law basis. But unfortunately there was a division of opinion between those six judges. One must concede that that is creating a majority by means of a technical reason. But Mabo, as I say, is an unfortunate example from our point of view – where you secure acceptance of a majority decision only by recourse to a technicality."

The key findings were made out in the lead judgment written by the Queenslander Sir Gerard Brennan, which included his reasoning as to why all precedents in Australian law of property should be overturned:

> "Whatever the justification advanced in earlier days for refusing to recognise the rights and interests in land of the indigenous inhabitants of settled colonies, an unjust and discriminatory doctrine of that kind can no longer be accepted. The expectations of the international community accord in this respect with the contemporary values of the Australian people."

Brennan was supported by Sir Anthony Mason and Michael McHugh. Their findings were varied somewhat, but still much supported, in the judgment written by Sydney's Sir William Deane and Mary Gaudron, and in the most Aborigine-friendly judgment by John Toohey, the one with some actual knowledge of Aborigines.

The odd-judge-out was Sir Daryl Dawson who wrote that *"if traditional land rights (or at least rights akin to them) are to be afforded to the inhabitants of the Murray Islands, the responsibility, both legal and moral, lies with the legislature and not with the courts"* – a view shared by a great many people outside the Court.

Here, in summary form, are the bare essentials of the decisions by those whom Hugh Morgan has labelled The Mabo Six:

> The **Meriam people** are entitled "against the whole of the world" to the possession, occupation, use and enjoyment of most of the island of Mer.
>
> The doctrine of **Terra Nullius** – that the land belonged to no one at the time of European settlement – is wrong. Justice Brennan, commenting that common law must not be "frozen

in an age of racial discrimination", wrote that "the Court can overrule the existing authorities, discarding the distinction between inhabited colonies that were *terra nullius* and those which were not."

Native Title does exist and can be protected by legal action; it may be held by an individual, group or community depending on "traditional laws and customs" which will be determined by the law of the indigenous people, not Australian law.

Native title can be **extinguished** in several ways:

1. When the traditional owners have moved or died;
2. When a valid grant of freehold title has been made;
3. In a majority of cases when a lease has been granted, including a mining lease (but not an exploration license);
4. When the Crown has used land for roads, railways or buildings such as post offices and the like.

Most claims for **Compensation** to native title-holders are rejected, except under certain terms of the *Racial Discrimination Act 1975* (as discussed when we covered *Mabo No. 1*).

The judgments raised as many questions as they provided answers, as events have shown ever since. The only response enjoying wide acceptance is that put, for one, by Peter Walsh who commented that *"nobody knows what the High Court might do next"* and went on, surely in sorrow:

"It is hard to understand how anyone could ever have seen the Court's unadumbrated Mabo decision as a formula for reconciliation, peace, harmony, nirvana or whatever. It is easy to see it as a prescription for making a few hundred more QCs multi-millionaires over a couple of decades of litigation."

He was echoed by McGuinness :

"There has to be a good deal of High Court litigation simply to force that Court to tidy up a lot of uncertainties the Mabo decision has created."

There was an interesting contribution from Greg McIntyre, the solicitor who rode the Mabo case from go to whoa:

"The process of consultation resolved upon by the Federal Cabinet may find a solution to easier cases. But the difficult ones will probably be decided in the courts."

And a succinct one from Jeffrey Kennett, Premier of Victoria:

"Mabo is going to be the lawyers' gravy train."

The wider reactions ran from bewilderment and doubt to anger. From the avalanche, I quote just five:

"Nobody knows what Mabo means...I used to think that the High Court was there to interpret the laws of the country and not have the legislators have to come back and interpret the law made by the High Court."
– *Ian McLachlan, Opposition spokesman on National Development*

"The Mabo decision has regrettably brought about greater confusion and uncertainty, not only for access for exploration, but in terms of potential costs of compensation, risks with existing titles and mechanisms for issuing of new titles."

— **Lauchlan McIntosh**, *Executive Director of the Australian Mining Industry Council*

"There is much difficulty in giving practical expression in our system of land law, and under our Constitution, to an assertion of ownership of land derived from a different legal system. The land in question is in effect subject to two incompatible legal structures."

— **Colin Howard**, *for twenty-six years Hearn Professor of Law at the University of Melbourne, now a member of the Victorian Bar*

"Those six High Court emperors (or in one case, empress) have, in this matter, no intellectual clothes."

— **John Stone**, *former head of Treasury and former Senator*

"As law, the decision is pitiful...This is naked assumption of power by a body quite unfitted to make the political and social decisions which are involved."

— **Peter Connolly QC**, *former judge of Supreme Court of Queensland, addressing the Samuel Griffith Society, named after the first Chief Justice.*

Such was the weight of complaints that the Chief Justice decided – and I'm sure he could properly do nothing less – to explain the decisions taken by the Court; indeed he did so on two occasions. First – in an interview with *Australian Lawyer*, the magazine of the Law Council of Australia – Sir Anthony denied that the Court had strayed beyond its jurisdiction and suggested Mabo was an example of how governments like to pass the buck:

> "In some circumstances governments and legislatures prefer to leave the determination of a controversial question to the courts rather than leave the question to be decided by the political process."

On the second occasion he went offshore, to a legal conference at Cambridge University. He demonstrated that he was neither thick skinned nor without humour. In the light of several controversial decisions by the Court over the last couple of years – the expulsion of independent member Phil Cleary from Parliament and the freedom-of-expression reversal of the government's ban on political advertising, as well as Mabo, come to mind – he said he could not recall any time during his career as a lawyer of such sustained criticism:

> "More disconcerting has been the concentrated campaign run by the mining industry, supported by the pastoral interests, to discredit our decision in relation to the Aboriginal land rights case, Mabo. That campaign has been conducted with a view to discrediting the decision and persuading the government to, in effect, repeal it and, if need be, even to initiate the constitutional processes that would result in an amendment to the Constitution."

He went on to whinge, surely naively, that this campaign...

> "Has convinced me that we live in an era in which what we are doing as judges will be the subject of public attention and debate. And that we must accustom ourselves to increasing and closer public scrutiny."

I should think so. The learned Justices have been insulated from public reaction for too long, up there in their ivory tower in a town which is one big ivory tower.

To give him his due, Sir Anthony regaled his audience at Cambridge with the incident when a Labor backbencher (Graeme Campbell, the member for Kalgoorlie) who was angered by the Court's action in expelling Cleary from Parliament, described it as a decision "by seven pissants":

> "It emerged that the word has two traditional English usages: one 'as drunk as a pissant'; two 'as game as a pissant'. The Australian vernacular usage was said to be a person 'who messes about'. The American vernacular was said to be a person 'who is incorrigible'. Having run the gauntlet of this abusive campaign, I came to the conclusion that the preferable meaning, when applied to a judge, is 'as game as a pissant'."

Game or not, Sir Anthony has shown himself capable of saying things which are chilling in their unworldly disregard for possible consequences. Try this one, cast after the Court's Mabo decision, through the *Australian Lawyer*:

> "The pursuit of the consequences flowing from a decision is not something that the Court can do anything about."

Chapter Eight

Keating II : Making His Mabo Play

When ad-man John Singleton gave Labor its fifth and unforeseen term by telling Keating to just keep plugging "Fifteen per cent GST", the new Prime Minister-in-his-own-right found himself with no policies to provide the million unemployed with work, no policies to check the ballooning national debt, no policies to turn round the deeply depressed economy.

All he had was his personal trinity: republican Australia; APEC – Asia Pacific Economic Co-Operation; Aboriginal reconciliation.

There can be no republic without a referendum and there is no way a referendum would succeed during Keating's political lifetime. There is no way, either, that Australia can lead the way on APEC – we can only follow the big boys. So that left the Aborigines as his only feathers to fly with.

That speech in Redfern three months before the election showed that he was more than ready to don the hair shirt, and that he saw the Mabo Judgment as a heaven-sent starting point. That is why he had these particular references put into the speech:

"By doing away with the bizarre conceit that this continent had no owners prior to the settlement of Europeans, Mabo establishes a fundamental truth and lays the basis for justice...Mabo is an historic decision – we can make it an historic turning point, the basis of a new relationship between indigenous and non-Aboriginal Australians...And if we have a sense of justice, as well as common sense, we will forge a new partnership."

There was very little of that sort of talk during the election campaign when he simply clung onto the Singleton GST mantra. But he had ordered a group of bureaucrats – led by Sandy Hollway, the first assistant secretary in the Department of Prime Minister and Cabinet – to work up proposals to discuss with Aboriginal representatives in the event of a miraculous win, and the government mapping service was secretly putting together a picture of what Aboriginal tribes occupied which pieces of land and to what they might be expected to lay claim.

Right after the allocation of portfolios in the newly-returned government, Keating picked up the Mabo baton and prepared to run with it. In the event, he soon ran into trouble.

Two ministers became direct assistants to him: Robert Tickner, heading Aboriginal Affairs who was shortly to declare – while wrapped in a traditional *lava lava* (sarong) on Thursday Island – that *"Mabo is the most important ethical and moral decision of our time"*; and Frank Walker, the Special Minister of State with responsibility inside the Prime Minister's office for advancing the Mabo issue, who had been Minister for Aboriginal Affairs for three years in the New South Wales government, and is a QC. (Walker later engaged as a special consultant Phillip Toyne, former head of the Australian Conservation Foundation and a prime member of the chattering classes.)

Keating press-ganged five more ministers into a special Mabo sub-committee of Cabinet: John Dawkins, the Treasurer; Ralph Willis, finance; Michael Lee, resources; Simon Crean, primary industries, and Michael Lavarch, the Attorney-General. When the new Cabinet met for the first time some three weeks after the election, Keating briefed them on Mabo developments and then quickly reduced it to a meeting of his Mabo eight.

Two matters were before them. One was the interdepartmental committee's interim report on the options available for dealing with Mabo (ranging from doing nothing to guaranteeing mining and pastoral leases by legislation). The other was a warning from a specially-formed coalition of eight peak business organisations – including the Australian Mining Industry Council, the Business Council of Australia and the Australian Chamber of Commerce and Industry – that doubts about property rights raised by the Mabo Judgment were already becoming a "major impediment" to investment; they called for the release of the bureaucrats' report for public discussion and for early government action. Keating responded that No, the report would not be opened for discussion because it was only at the development stage, and No, the government would not make any hasty moves. He also said there would be a full meeting with Aboriginal leaders within weeks.

In preparation for that meeting the bureaucrats polished up their options report, and influential Aborigines held a strategy meeting at Alice Springs. The Aborigines saw in Keating's declared goal of a "historic reconciliation" a fine opportunity to stake claims of considerable proportions.

So, when some thirty Aborigines met with the Mabo committee of ministers in Canberra at 11 o'clock on Tuesday, 27 April 1993, they presented four pages of "Notes". (These notes were thereafter called "The Aboriginal Peace Plan" in material given out by ATSIC – the Aboriginal and Torres Strait Islander Commission – and in statements by the more notable or publicity-seeking Aborigines.)

The notes called for immediate legislation which would, among many other things, *"recognise and affirm"* Aborigines' rights *"wherever they may exist"*; ensure that Aborigines' rights *"are not extinguished by past and future grants"* by the Crown; set up a tribunal to issue declarations of Aboriginal title on grounds of *"common law, historical* *association or **needs***" (my emphasis on the word 'needs'); and establish a Settlement Process to resolve by negotiation all Aboriginal *"interests and rights"* including a land acquisition fund, ownership and management of resources (mining), hunting and fishing rights, plus *"constitutional arrangements"* and **"self government"** (again my emphasis).

A good deal of hoop-la surrounded this first meeting, television cameras aplenty and reporters all over the place. Nearly everyone who considered themselves someone in Aboriginal politics were there: Lois O'Donoghue, chair of ATSIC; Pat Dodson, chair of the Council for Aboriginal Reconciliation; Tauto Sansbury, chair of the South Australian Aboriginal Legal Rights Movement; Ted Wilkes, chair of the Western Australian Aboriginal Legal Service, and the chairs of the several Land Councils: Galarrwuy Yunupingu of the Northern, Bruce Breadon of the Central, John Watson of the Kimberley, Jean George of the Cape York, and Manul Ritchie of New South Wales.

Even this spread did not satisfy everybody. Pat O'Shane, the prominent woman Aboriginal activist and magistrate in New South Wales, complained that Keating's reconciliation drive had become a *"gabfest"* and an *"expensive fraud"* and that the Mabo process had been *"hijacked by bureaucrats"* in ATSIC. Mary Graham, a lecturer and a Queensland member of the Council for Aboriginal Reconciliation, said she had received many phone calls, most of them from urban Aborigines, protesting that the group being consulted was too narrow and that the process was too secretive and too rushed. And Father Frank Brennan, a son of the High Court's Brennan and head of the Jesuit-financed Uniya Centre for social research, said that *"there must come a stage where the government can sit down with Aboriginal representatives who are broadly legitimate in terms of the various Aboriginal groups and who can come to the table with the peak mining and pastoral bodies."*

That is easier said than done. One great difficulty is that

there are more than five hundred different tribes or groups, some of them very small but all jealously guarding their individuality. There is no true national Aboriginal structure, and many who claim to speak for all Aborigines are charlatans and know it!

Keating made things worse when he tried to progress matters with a more compact group a few weeks after that show conference. He and his Mabo ministers met with just five: Michael Dodson, the recently-appointed Commissioner for Aboriginal Social Justice and former director of the Northern Land Council and the Aborigine Keating most turned to for advice; Noel Pearson, organiser of the Cape York Land Council; Rob Riley, a former clerk of courts and soldier who has spent years as executive officer of the Aboriginal Legal Service in Western Australia and as chairman of the National Aboriginal Conference; Sandra Saunders, the director of the South Australian Aboriginal Legal Rights Movement; and their legal representative, Ron Castan, QC.

It was Castan who made the front running, thoroughly irritating Keating who neither fancies being lectured by lawyers nor reacts kindly to strident demands. He soon lost patience with his visitors' refusal to compromise and the meeting broke up.

Even so, as became clear later, Keating did give certain undertakings at one or both of his meetings – promises which were to bedevil his negotiations with the States.

Noel Pearson, who attended the two meetings with the Mabo ministers, found that there were two quite different attitudes to the process. The bureaucrats, whose reports formed the bases of the ministerial approach, saw it as a land management matter. The Aborigines saw it as a need to recognise their human rights. Pearson wrote:

> "The IDC's (inter-departmental committee's) principles offer a continuation of the colonial legacy with whites free to take from blacks as they please and without regard to the relationship to the land developed over millennia that is at the heart of Aboriginal title."

And, reflecting the optimistic hopes that had been built up in many Aborigines, he went a good deal further:

> "So much has been lost that Aboriginal people are entitled to expect special protection for what remains. There needs to be positive acknowledgement of *different* (his italics) treatment of Aboriginal title which reflects the fact that Aboriginal culture is inseparable from the land to which Aboriginal title attaches. The loss or impairment of that title is not simply a loss of real estate, it is a loss of culture."

Clearly, Keating was facing difficulties. Aborigines were starting to voice their doubts about him. He was able to stem the tide a little during a nose-rubbing welcome by Maoris to Auckland, New Zealand, where he announced that, in response to the Mabo Judgment...

> "The government of Australia and the governments of the States are seeking to put into a body of law a native title for the indigenous peoples of Australia...This can and must be the first effective basis of reconciliation between Aboriginal people and non- Aboriginal Australians."

If this did rekindle flagging hopes, Keating and his side-kick Walker soon doused them with what the Aborigines saw as a swift act of betrayal.

It concerned a massive mineral deposit with the unlikely name of Here's Your Chance which was discovered nearly forty years ago on the land of the small Kurdanji tribe beside the McArthur River in the Northern Territory, south of the Gulf of Carpentaria. It needed vastly improved mining techniques to make it viable. When they were achieved by 1990-91 a joint venture was formed to develop the project at a cost of $250 million. MIM Holdings – launched as Mt Isa Mines in 1926 to extract base metals in far-western Queensland and today an international mining and metals giant – holds 72 per cent with the balance in the hands of four Japanese companies: Nippon Mining and Metals, Mitsui, Mitsubishi Materials and Marubeni. The Commonwealth put in $5.9 million and the Northern Territory $10 million to build roads and upgrade the airport at nearby Borroloola. The leases, approvals and environmental red tape were tidied into the Northern Territory's *McArthur River Project Agreement Ratification Act* and it was confidently predicted that, when developed, the job would yield 160,000 tonnes of zinc, 45,000 tonnes of lead and 1.6 million ounces of silver, earning a net return to Australia of some $200 million a year, and employing about two hundred and fifty people both during and after construction.

Then came the spectre of Mabo, the risk that land-rights claims might stall the whole undertaking. Northern Territory chief minister Marshall Perron, a former tally clerk and tugboat operator, wrote in anguish to Keating:

> "The joint-venture partners have indicated that unless they can be assured of certainty of title in time to commence operations by July 1, the project will be delayed indefinitely."

Keating and Walker gave Perron the written backing he required – guarantees that they would legislate if necessary to support water-tightening amendments to the *McArthur Ratification Act* and promising to pay any legal costs incurred by the Territory in fighting off any challenges.

Aborigines were furious. Brett Midena, acting director of the Northern Land Council, foreshadowed a challenge and complained: *"They are legislating to protect the rights of a company but not the rights of Aboriginal people. The (amending) Bill represents a total denial of natural justice."* Lois O'Donoghue, chair of ATSIC, growled: *"The deals apparently done between the Commonwealth and the Northern Territory effectively undermined the Aboriginal community's bargaining position."* And the government's own representative on the Council for Aboriginal Reconciliation, the Left's Senator Margaret Reynolds, protested: *"This has jeopardised the hard-won, patient and positive atmosphere in the Mabo negotiations... It's timing undermines the faith we all have in the process."*

Within forty-eight hours Keating was on ABC television's *Four Corners* protesting the predicament he had got himself into:

> "Were the project not to proceed, you can imagine the noise which would be around. People would be saying: 'Well, here's Mabo; at first blush a $300 million (sic) project hits the fence.' You'd have the worst elements of conservative interests in this country up there blackguarding the Mabo decision and what it stands for."

At this time he was making final plans for a meeting with all the Premiers the following week, a conference pompously dubbed the Council of Australian Governments (COAG). Those preparations included dispatch to the Premiers – only days ahead of the time set for its adoption – of the latest version of the bureaucrats' response to the Mabo Judgment, which had been accepted by the full Cabinet. It contained a roll of so-called principles which Keating expected to dragoon the Premiers into accepting as a platform for action. As is usually the case with public-servants' prose, the thirty-three principles easily come down to half a dozen paragraphs:

> **Identification of Native Title:** "It is desirable to establish a better means than the courts for determining who has native title and where. The system should be accessible, informal, non-adversarial and expeditious. A tribunal system has attractions...Governments should provide adequate resources for the tribunal process."
>
> **Principle of Non-Discrimination:** "Native title should be treated no less favourably than other comparable titles."

Protection of Native Title: "Native title should be preserved to the maximum extent possible. The common law should be amended to provide that grants should not themselves extinguish native title...Where possible native title should revive at the expiry of a finite grant."

Transition to the New Regime: "Those holding grants of interests in land should have certainty that they will not be invalidated and their rights should be protected. The Government is willing to legislate to facilitate the validation of post-1975 *(since the Racial Discrimination Act)* grants by the States and Territories subject to appropriate compensation being paid...A cut-off date of 30 June 1993 is to be set whereby, in respect of grants after that date, the Commonwealth will not in the normal course facilitate, support validation or provide compensation...A future grant of interest should be subject to the consent of the native title holders in relation to actions affecting their land" *(i.e. possible veto against mining).*

Compensation: "Legislation should establish parameters for compensation when a grant is made over native title land, rather than leaving this for resolution by the courts. This could set out broad principles or a specific scheme for calculation of compensation."

Justice and Economic Development: "A response is needed which addresses past dispossession, as a consequence of which many Aboriginal and Torres Strait Island people cannot now benefit from Mabo, and also the desirability of reducing conflict between (native) land holders and resource development...perhaps through a revenue equivalents scheme."

It was a program to please no one.

The Australian Mining Industry Council's acting director, Geoff Ewing, said that by saying Aboriginal title should *"revive"* after a mining lease had run out, the government had *"taken a quantum leap in expanding the High Court's decision and, therefore, the uncertainty that flows from it"* and, by not putting a time limit on the lodging of Mabo-style claims, *"companies would never know where claims would be coming from."*

The National Farmers Federation executive director, Rick Farley, echoed the objection to revival of native title: *"It goes well beyond the High Court decision. The grant of a pastoral lease extinguishes native title."*

People who might be said to occupy the middle ground, such as Father Brennan, found that it failed to deliver a broader reconciliation: *"It will not be enough to kick-start the sort of just and proper settlement Paul Keating has been speaking of."*

And Aborigines, among whom – as the *Financial Review's* Canberra correspondent Tom Burton observed – *"Keating's public comments have fired up huge expectations"*, reacted with disappointment bordering on disgust.

Noel Pearson, of the Cape York Land Council, dismissed the paper as a *"fairly slimey, useless document"* and Mick Dodson, who Keating had consulted frequently, washed his hands of it:

> "We reject any suggestion that the discussion paper or the principles are the product of negotiation with the indigenous people of this country."

The Premiers arrived for the Melbourne meeting with a variety of views. New South Wales' John Fahey (Liberal) Queensland's Wayne Goss (Labor) and South Australia's Lynn Arnold (Labor) were broadly prepared to go along with Keating. Fahey wanted fast title resolution to stop "developing hysteria" while Goss was after a national compensation scheme rather than individual companies, graziers or States having to pay. Victoria's Jeff Kennett, Western Australia's Richard Court and Tasmania's Ray

Groom (all Liberal) were worried about threats of a right of veto over future mining and pastoral leases; but they, too, wanted an answer to what Kennett called *"a curious judgment of the High Court that goes nowhere but to a melting pot of confusion."*

The conference started badly for Keating and got worse. He opted to dodge the cameras and reporters by entering Victoria's labyrinthine Parliament House by the back way. He found himself waiting for a lift which did not respond to the call button. Eventually a cleaner pointed his party towards a flight of stairs and they trooped up to find that the meeting was convening in the room used by the Liberal Party!

Keating's staff had revised the thirty-three principles of the discussion paper down to eleven proposals which included the right of Aboriginal title holders to veto certain future mining ventures. But when discussion opened, three of the Liberal Premiers argued the basic point that native title as envisioned by the High Court could and should be legislated away.

Court said that if Keating's proposals were accepted, investment and exploration in Western Australia would stop and the State would become ungovernable – *"we would have to shut the front door."* Of Keating's view that the Mabo Judgment is *"sacrosanct"*, he said: *"It's all very well for you to say the judgment has been made, but WE are the legislators."* And Groom echoed him: *"It is very sad for this country if elected governments don't have control."*

Kennett said that *"the only way in which we will have another dollar spent in this country"* is by redefining native title in legislation which allows Aborigines less control over land use in return for compensation.

Keating told the Premiers that the Mabo judgment *"made seminal changes to the way the world is. Either you face up to it. Or you adopt a sledgehammer approach which I do not think is right, just or equitable."*

Kennett responded that the Mabo Judgment discriminated against the majority of Australians. *"Which Australians?"* Treasurer Dawkins interjected. *"Seventeen-and-a-half* million people," Kennett shot back, *"and you are discriminating against them to give special treatment to Aborigines."*

Keating reacted angrily: *"The point is to even up – not to provide something extra for one group of people... We came into Port Jackson a couple of hundred years ago with a dozen ships and took everything away. Mabo starts to redress that."*

After two hours of such exchanges the attendant officials were invited to leave – some of them to deal with a group of Aborigines who were demonstrating on the steps with their flag and demanding admittance. *"We believe that our interests are being debated away behind the walls of Parliament while Aboriginal people have no opportunity to put their case,"* said Geoff Clark, administrator of the Framlingham (in the western district of Victoria) Aboriginal Trust. *"We are here to negotiate with government."* But the officials, having received a deputation of two, turned them away.

The Premiers argued all day and into the night. Then, some time after ten o'clock, Kennett announced that, given that there was no sign of agreement, he would do his own legislating: *"I am not trying to be difficult, but the solution suggested by the Commonwealth is unacceptable."* So saying he stood up and walked out. The others followed. And Keating was obliged to ponder how he might rescue his situation on the morrow.

In the event he returned to the table with what he called a "very generous offer." After making a patronising gibe about "Jeff's little pantomime", he spelled it out:

> "Canberra offered to pay ALL the compensation which might arise under the *Racial Discrimination Act 1975* from native titles having been extinguished.
>
> Canberra offered to limit the veto rights of Aborigines over access to land and mining.
>
> Canberra offered to abandon revival of native title after pastoral, tourism or residential leases had expired and limit revival after mining."

These provided grounds for good and lengthy discussion and progress was made. Just how much progress depends on whom you listened to.

It is a fact that the second and last day of the conference broke up in acrimony. But why?

> Keating: "Responsibility for the failure of this meeting to agree on a national response rests largely with Premiers Kennett and Court because of their refusal to accept that the High Court has actually made a decision which required a process and a mechanism to give effect to that process. I gave substantial ground but they wouldn't give any."

But those of us who listened to the ABC's radio program *AM* next morning heard Kennett and Court describe in some detail another scenario. Their version was that an agreement had been hammered out by all concerned. But while Kennett's staff were typing it up, Keating went into a closed meeting with his advisers. When he emerged it was to say that they must agree to his total package. Court recalled that Keating said: *"If you don't accept my principles, well that's it, buster."*

The morning papers also carried Kennett saying: *"We wanted to walk one step at a time. The Prime Minister wanted to do it all at once... He wanted to go beyond the High Court decision to resolve the whole so-called Aboriginal question. He was there to take on board his concept of guilt and what's happened in this country since settlement...He was using Balmain thuggery."*

The Keating version got the bigger play, probably because members of the Canberra press gallery who covered the story make their living out of news provided by government and will not risk becoming *persona non grata* with its boss. But it is unlikely, to say the least that, with a room full of witnesses, Kennett and Court would have been parsimonious with the truth.

The likelihood was that, at that last-minute talk with his minders, Keating was reminded of his promises to the Aborigines and advised that the lesser agreement he had reached with the Premiers would not be acceptable to them.

Anyway, soon afterwards he took a fast plane to China, leaving Mabo in limbo.

Newspoll on a national basis and a Morgan Opinion Poll in Victoria asked people what they were thinking about Mabo in the week following the Melbourne fiasco. In both, a majority of people who expressed an opinion were opposed to Aborigines being able to claim native title to land, more markedly so in Victoria – against in Newspoll 52 per cent, in Morgan 57 per cent. Similarly, a majority of those with a view were opposed to compensation being paid for use of Aboriginal land, again more strongly in Victoria – against in Newspoll 57 per cent, in Morgan 66 per cent.

Morgan asked this interesting question: *"Do you, yourself, feel any personal guilt over the treatment of Victorian Aborigines in the two hundred years since British settlement, or not?"* Among all electors the result was Yes 29 per cent, No 67 per cent and Can't Say 4 per cent; among Labor voters the percentage of Nos was even higher, 69 per cent. Paul Keating, eat your heart out.

Chapter Nine

Give Us Land, Lots Of It

"The risk is that for some people Mabo has turned into a kind of cargo cult. Some seem to think that Mabo will deliver the sophisticated consumer goods, the fantasy of tribal life, the independent Aboriginal State they have persuaded themselves to believe in. These are serious mistakes."

– *The Australian, 5 June 1993*

All the Keating rhetoric about reconciliation and a marvellous tomorrow naturally led many Aborigines to expect pie in the sky or, specifically, thousands of broad acres to call their own. When the first anniversary of the Mabo Judgment rolled round, Mabo-induced land claims generated by the Aboriginal Industry were thudding into the courts. So many of them indeed that Minister Tickner – who usually, as Northern Territory Premier Perron so rightly said, *"either supports outrageous claims or deafens us with his silence"* – was obliged to issue a warning to most of the claimants:

"They haven't got a legal feather to fly with. Their chances of success are nil. It is mischievous for lawyers to suggest to Aboriginal people that dispossessed people are going to have any prospect of obtaining land-rights justice under Mabo."

He had a silly shot at the media on the way through, too:

"It is just extraordinary and reprehensible that so many so-called newspapers have reported these claims as holy writ."

Events showed that few Aborigines were prepared to heed him. Let us make a clockwise round-the-nation survey, starting in...

Victoria: The Yorta Yorta people – advised by Castan QC and Keon-Cohen, two of the barristers who successfully argued the Mabo case – lodged a claim in the Melbourne office of the High Court for some 50,000 hectares of vacant Crown property, wetlands and forests on both sides of the Murray River, stretching westwards from Tocumwal to Cohuna.

There are a thousand to fifteen hundred in the tribe today, two hundred of them living in a settlement near Barmah at the centre of their claim; conceivably some five hundred generations of their forbears cut canoes from the giant river red gums which are a feature of the area. The writ, in the names of five of the tribe, said the Yorta Yorta have been in uninterrupted possession of the land; it also sought compensation for damages caused by logging, cattle grazing and tourist activities and for impairment of native title, naming Victoria and New South Wales as defendants.

Five other Aboriginal communities in Victoria were considering lodging claims to native title.

Tasmania: Peter Rae, a former Liberal Senator and a lawyer practising in Launceston, lodged a High Court claim for one-hundred-and-twenty-six hectares and the settlement of Wybalenna on Flinders Island, at the eastern end of Bass Strait, on behalf of three descendants of Mannalargenna, the last chief of the Portland tribe. One-hundred-and-fifty of the island's nine hundred residents are officially listed as Aborigines.

It is hard to imagine that any claims could be lodged for land on Tasmania proper because history books are full of the fact that its last Aborigine, Truganini, died in Hobart on 8 May, 1876. But the activist Michael Mansell, secretary of the self-styled Aboriginal Provisional Government, announced he was preparing a claim for 20 per cent of the State's land. He further asserted that all vacant Crown land throughout Australia should be handed to Aborigines along with the $6 billion which, he said, is raised from Crown land in rents and royalties!

South Australia: Malcolm Champion, a spokesman for the powerful Pitjantjatjara people, said claims within the State would fail because Aboriginal groups could not agree who the land belonged to originally: *"Because of government red tape, the present boundaries have divided groups and families... The urbanised and traditional people are divided because the tribal people have already got land and the urbanised people haven't."*

To bear him out, the Arabunna people and the Dieri Association could not agree which should occupy Finnis Springs pastoral station – 1,492 square kilometres about 1,000 kilometres north of Adelaide – whose lease was resumed by the government in 1992. While that dispute dragged on, lawyers acting for the Arabunna, lodged a Mabo-style claim for vast nearby tracts of land – as big as Tasmania – embracing Lake Eyre, the old stock-route stopovers of Maree and Oodnadatta and fourteen pastoral properties including the 13,986 square kilometres of Anna Creek, the world's largest cattle station. The only problem was that an error in the documents extended the claim to parts of Africa and South America as well.

Caught in the middle of these claims was Western Mining's $1 billion Olympic Dam operation at Roxby Downs which produces 70,000 tonnes of copper, 1,370 tonnes of uranium oxide and 32,000 ounces of gold a year. One claim included the mine's township, the other covered the vital sources of water.

Western Australia: This State was in a mess before Mabo made it worse. Forty-four per cent of its land – that's more than a million square kilometres, bigger than New South Wales and Victoria combined, much bigger than Texas and nearly five times bigger than the United Kingdom – was closed permanently or for the time being to both mineral exploration and mining, yet the mining industry generates more than $12 billion of the West's annual revenue!

The locked-up areas were a combination of Aboriginal reserves, Aboriginal sites (there are up to 750,000 sacred sites alone!), national parks (60 of them), nature conservation reserves, proposed conservation reserves, state forests, national estate listings and world heritage listings – there is a plan to have the entire Nullarbor Plain given world heritage listing under federal law which overrides state law!

Then when the Mabo Judgment was handed down, Peter Ellery, chief executive of the West Australian Chamber of Mines and Energy, estimated that more than 80 per cent of the State – *that's over two million square kilometres* – was thrown open to native-title claims because it was Crown land or Crown leases and Aborigines did have some abiding associations with much of it.

No wonder that Premier Richard Court – reflecting the very real anxieties and anger of his electorate – has been the loudest in his protests against Keating's schemes to enlarge Mabo and most insistent in demanding a national referendum on the matter.

Fantastic frustration is exemplified in the case of the Rudall River Moratorium Zone which has seen Australia's biggest company, BHP, and the fifth-biggest, CRA, kept in balk for six years. They sought to explore the potential El Dorado – which is in the Great Sandy Desert some 500 kilometres south-east of Port Hedland and lies between the Rudall River and the Canning Stock Route – back in the 1980s; they were fully aware, of course, that gold and copper were being mined not far away and uranium had been discovered.

But in 1987, in response to heritage and cultural claims by the Punmu community and the Parngurr people who had decided to move in, the Burke Labor government declared an exploration exclusion zone which was to last for five years at the most. Instead, in 1991, it was extended to blanket an area of 70,000 square kilometres. And last year a little-known group, the Rudall River Task Force, successfully recommended to Dr Carmen Lawrence's Labor government that the exploration moratorium should continue. Then, in the autumn of 1993, the local communities made an application through the Aboriginal Legal Service in Perth for a Mabo-style claim on the land.

Further north, the Kimberley Land Council instituted another Mabo-inspired claim on behalf of the Burunga, who asserted tribal links with the sea skirting the area, for 20,000 square kilometres north of One Arm Point; Kimberley pastoral leaseholders were immediately obliged to engage legal help which they could not easily afford, while the Aborigines' lawyers were funded by taxpayers.

And a group of elders, no doubt filled with Mabo euphoria, took out a Supreme Court writ challenging the repeal at the turn of the century of Section 70 of the Western Australia Constitution, which said that £5,000 pounds or 1 per cent of the State's annual revenues – which ever was the higher – must be set aside for the welfare of Aborigines. They were keen to get their hands on that 1 per cent which today would be about $600 million a year! Like most of the Mabo claimants, their chances had to be rated as very slim.

Northern Territory: If Western Australia has been largely locked up, you would have to say the Territory has been throttled by the Whitlam-inspired and Fraser-instituted *Aboriginal Land Rights (Northern Territory) Act 1976.* Roughly half of the Territory is now in Aboriginal hands or being claimed which means, under the Act, that it is controlled by the Land Councils.

Campbell Anderson, managing director of Renison Goldfields Consolidated (which, among other vast operations, still works the old gold-rush field at Pine Creek north of Katherine) and president of the Australian Mining Industry Council, has put the position clearly:

> "Aboriginal owners, or those representing them, cannot only demand unlimited compensation for the mining stage but can impose unrealistic conditions as a price for initial access. These rights have almost frozen exploration and no new mine has been developed on any Aboriginal land since the commencement of the Act...
>
> "To March 1993 the Northern Territory Mines Minister had received 544 applications for exploration licenses on Aboriginal land. The Minister consented to negotiate 403 (74 per cent) of these, but the Aboriginal Land Councils consented to only 43 (8 per cent).
>
> "This means that companies which would otherwise have been happy to operate in the Territory have spent their exploration dollars elsewhere."

The power of the Land Councils was put to the test almost exactly a year after the Mabo Judgment, not by the mining industry but by a hundred Aborigines of the Aranda tribe who did not want to have their land administered by the Central Land Council, based in Alice Springs.

The land lies between the King's Canyon National Park and Lake Amadeus, about 300 kilometres west of Alice springs and 80 kilometres north of Ayers Rock. Aboriginal Affairs Minister Tickner planned, under the *Land Rights Act*, to grant the land to a trust run by the Land Council. But the Aranda, in the name of four of its women, sought to stop him under a Mabo-style claim, their solicitor, Jane MacPherson, reasoning that the judge-made law took precedence over the Act.

The collision between the Mabo Judgment and the

established law was argued before the full bench of the Federal Court in Sydney. Alan Sullivan QC, for the tribe, said the Act worked to *"destroy"* the concept of native title recognised in Mabo; the Act set up a *"bureaucratic regime"* under which the Land Council managed the land whereas under Mabo the native title holders could be *"as wise or foolish, as altruistic or selfish"*. Ian Barker QC, for Tickner and two nominated members of the Council, maintained that *"what is sought here is to bring down a major socially-beneficial piece of legislation…and wreck a system which has worked to the benefit of Northern Territory Aborigines."* The court reserved its decision and (at the time of writing) has still to hand down its finding. It will clearly be a significant one.

Queensland: The interesting figure of Castan QC, who led for Mabo in the High Court and has long been into Aboriginal matters, is prominent again in the most significant claim of all, the grab for land round the huge bauxite operation on Cape York Peninsula, a grab threatening projects worth billions.

The target was not simply the land south of Weipa – on the east coast of the Gulf of Carpentaria and two-hundred-and-fifty kilometres below the tip of Cape York itself – but also the minerals beneath, in this case the world's biggest deposits of metal-grade bauxite from which aluminium is made. Hitherto and throughout Australia, minerals in the ground were and are the property of the Crown – of all the people.

Castan was briefed by Lyons, a leading firm of solicitors in Brisbane, who had been instructed a year earlier – soon after the main Mabo Judgment – by representatives of the Wik people's clans centred on the township of Aurukun seventy-five kilometres south of Weipa. There was no way the claim was fanciful because, as Geoffrey Ewing of the Mining Industry Council said on ABC radio: *"It's signed by Ron Castan, a reputable QC who wouldn't have signed unless he thought there was an arguable case."*

(In his role as Human Rights and Equal Opportunity Commissioner and not long after lodging the Weipa claim, Castan fined a couple $20,700 for declining to rent a caravan to two Aboriginals. He commented: *"This it as a serious and significant case of blatant racial discrimination occurring in an environment in which members of the community, including those handling rental accommodation, apparently regarded it as acceptable to refuse accommodation to Aboriginal people."* He broke the fine into $700 for economic loss and $20,000 for pain, humiliation, distress and loss of personal dignity.)

We will go into the thinking behind the claim in a moment. But the real-estate grab was for some 35,000 square kilometres and, as well as rich mineral deposits not yet worked, it embraced the Archer Bend and Rokeby national parks and the settlements of Napranum near Weipa and Pormpuaaw on the site of the old Edward River mission some two hundred kilometres to the south – indeed it amounted to more than half of all Cape York Peninsula north of the 15th parallel.

The rusty-red bauxite cliffs of Weipa had first been noted (but not recognised as valuable) in 1802 in the fine charts drawn by Matthew Flinders, then aged twenty-eight, when he was the first to sail right round Australia. Apart from the Presbyterians opening a mission at Weipa, nothing much happened for one-hundred-and-fifty years when Maurice Mawby, shrewdest of mining men and boss of the $8 billion-plus CRA, suggested a geologist take a good look at Cape York.

Harold Evans took up the challenge in 1955. With an Aboriginal companion from the mission, he set out in a (very cramped) three-metre fibreglass dinghy, sailing into amazement: *"The journey down the coast revealed miles of bauxite cliffs"* – in fact about a quarter of all the world's known resources of the stuff!

The Queensland government passed an Act in 1957 which allowed mine development to start the following year. Comalco Limited was formed, originally with CRA in a joint venture with Kaiser Aluminium of America, and work began. At the same time a big co-operative refining plant was built at Gladstone, on the east coast near Rockhampton. When it was ready the bauxite from Weipa was turned into alumina (aluminium oxide) and then shipped on to smelters either in Tasmania (cheap hydro power for the heavy supplies of electricity required) or the United States. By 1968, Blainey says, this was *"the costliest venture in the history of Australian mining."*

The major target of the Wik-Lyons-Castan claim is Comalco, now owned as to 67 per cent by CRA. And there are eight other respondents, including another mining company, the Commonwealth and Queensland governments, the Aboriginal and Torres Strait Islander Commission (ATSIC), three local Aboriginal community councils and one pastoral leaseholder who is an Aborigine. It was carefully and expensively put together; the solicitors plus an anthropologist covered the area collecting signatures from 185 claimants – some of whom said later they did not know what they were putting their names to, according to reporters Robyn Dixon of *The Age* and Jamie Walker of *The Australian.*

The thinking went something like this: The Mabo Judgment said that native title existed before settlement. Therefore, when Queensland legislated to lease the land to Comalco, it was owned by the Wik clans and the government had a fiduciary duty of trust and was not entitled to enter into agreements covering the area without the consent of the Aborigines. If that be so, Comalco's agreement with Queensland and its mining lease ML7,024 are invalid. (It could possibly mean that every other lease in Australia is invalid, too – which is what makes this case so crucial.)

The action launched in the Federal Court in Brisbane said that *"Comalco is, and at all material times, has been a trespasser without lawful entitlement upon the areas"* and sought damages as well as an injunction *"restraining Comalco from continuing to pursue any or all of its alleged rights"* to mine.

Comalco said it would *"defend the claim vigorously and, on the basis of advice available to us, we believe our titles will be found to be valid."* They were assured of support by Wayne Goss, Queensland's Labor Premier, although his Canberra colleagues demurred at first, with Keating mocking Goss for *"running to mamma".* But a spirited revolt inside Cabinet obliged him to eat crow. Keating undertook not only to support Comalco but to validate ALL titles back to 1788, and to do so with speed. Several of his ministers were alarmed by a declaration from John Ralph, chief executive of CRA and chairman of Comalco. He said that plans to spend $1.7 billion on buying the Gladstone power station from the Queensland government and up-grading the smelter Comalco had built at nearby Boyne Island might have to be called off. He told the ABC's *7.30 Report*:

> "If claims over the Weipa leases are still existing at the 31st December (1993), then that program will have to be deferred or not take place at all."

He added soon afterwards that there was no way international bankers would proceed when a legal action was poised over Weipa. Ralph had good grounds to be thoroughly fed up with Mabo. As we have seen, he was being frustrated in Western Australia and he had an earlier aggravation in Queensland. CRA planned to develop 118 million tonnes of ore, carrying zinc, led and silver, at the Century project, due south of Point Parker in the Gulf of Carpentaria. For two years an offer by CRA to survey sacred sites (in order to avoid doing any damage to them) had been held up by some of the Gungalidda tribe, while other members wanted to press ahead with the mine which would give work to some 700, and still others sought to pursue a Mabo-style claim over pastoral properties Lawn Hill and Pendine which CRA had purchased and over Konka station on which CRA had an option to buy. A decision whether or not to go ahead with the $750 million Century project was scheduled for early 1994, but has now been postponed.

Wild claims began in Queensland just six months after the Mabo Judgment was handed down. The Mullenjarli people started it; they decided to seek, through the South-East Queensland Aboriginal Legal Service (taxpayer funded, of course) a substantial section of Brisbane's central business district and a strip of land beside the Brisbane River running down to its mouth. Then the 4,000-

strong Bidjara tribe lodged a statement of claim covering the spectacular Carnarvon Range in central Queensland which attracts thousands of tourists every week. Six thousand descendants of the Dalungbara, Ngulungbara and Batchala tribes proclaimed their rights over Fraser Island, Lady Elliott Island and others in the Bunker Group off the mid-Queensland coast. And the Gubbi Gubbi Land and Cultural Association lodged a claim in the Supreme Court for tracts of the Sunshine Coast including Bribie Island.

New South Wales : The Wiradjuri people did nothing by halves when they laid claim in the High Court to most of the land pastoral, agricultural, horticultural and, indeed, urban – lying between the Lachlan River to the north and the Murrumbidgee River to the south. They were advised by barrister Paul Coe, who runs the aggressive National Aboriginal and Islander Legal Service from an office in Redfern and who told *Sixty Minutes*:

> "I think we are very moderate...They try to coerce us to go back onto the mission stations, to shut our mouths and to shut our minds. But now the blinkers are off, our minds are open, we think for ourselves, and we are capable of making up our own minds."

Guided by Coe, the Wiradjuri not only sought native title to all the land, but sovereignty as well, prompting a partner in law-firm Minter Ellison Morris Fletcher, John Mulally, to opine:

> "The Mabo decision would pale into insignificance compared to a successful Wiradjuri claim to sovereignty. If existing ownership titles are held to be invalid, then the existing ownership of every home, every farm, every school, every hospital and all other land will be invalid, or at least significantly prejudiced."

(Someone secured paper with the Wiradjuri letterhead and wrote phoney letters to several farm families in the Albury-Wodonga area asking them to share their home with Aborigines pending the outcome of the claim.)

The 250 descendants of the Wadi Wadi tribe lobbed a claim for the Wollongong-Illawarra coastal area, stretching from Helensburgh in the north to Nowra in the south and far enough inland to take in Moss Vale, Bowral and Mittagong.

And in Canberra a claim was lodged under Coe's counselling in the name of the Ngunnawal, Walgalu, Djilamatang and Ngarigo tribes for all the land between the Wiradjuri and Wadi Wadi claims, including all the **Australian Capital Territory** and Mount Kosciusko, and stretching down to the Victorian border. The High Court writ claimed valid title to the land plus compensation for its illegal use, and alleged that the Ngunnawal and *"related black nations"* had been subjected to...

> "Rape, kidnapping, pillage, murder, the systematic and unsystematic destruction of Aboriginal culture and other acts of unutterable shame."

Whatever merits the mounting number of claims might have, it has to be said that, when it comes to telling the tale, Coe and his colleagues in the various branches of the Aboriginal Legal Service are rarely guilty of under-stating their case.

Chapter Ten

Investors Go On Strike

They poured the first gold ingot at Mount Todd just a year after the Jawoyn said to the would-be miners: *"You'd better come and talk to us or we will put a Mabo style claim on you."* In that case, discussion worked.

The Mount Todd deal involved several interesting factors. The location – a massive reef of ore bearing up to an estimated $1 billion worth of gold – is about 40 kilometres north of the Katherine Gorge, a tourists' favourite in the Northern Territory, and 300 kilometres south-east by road from Darwin. The Aborigines are the same Jawoyn whose objections on grounds of religion and custom led Bob Hawke into his humiliating closure of Coronation Hill, and the people who secured repossession of the Gorge in 1989 and restored their name for it, *Nitmiluk*, which means "cicada dreaming." The company, Zapopan N.L., is wise in the ways of working with Aborigines from its experiences with the Walpiri in the red centre's Tanami Desert where it operates another gold mine which is ending its productive run.

In December 1992 John Ah Kit – executive officer of the Jawoyn Association who grew up smart in Darwin – offered, in addition to his talk-to-us-or-else ultimatum, to waive any claim to native title, damages or compensation on the mine-site itself in return for a package of some 5,000 square kilometres of land (made up of the rest of the Werenbun-Barnjarn pastoral lease, which surrounds the mine, the Eva Valley pastoral freehold and other properties) which immediately doubled the size of the Nitmiluk National Park, plus guarantees of jobs, training, houses and other benefits.

It was all put into an agreement which was signed in January 1993 by the Jawoyn Association, Zapopan and the Commonwealth and Territory governments. Terry Strapp, executive chairman of Perth-based Zapopan, told Rosemary West of *The Age*:

> "We are not intimidated by the Aboriginal people or Mabo. (Some other companies) felt we had sold the mining industry out. We say that's nonsense. The agreement is responsible to the Zapopan shareholders and responsible to the Jawoyn."

Certainly his shareholders had no ground for complaint; Zapopan's share price has trebled. The Jawoyn have been rewarded, too, with three times the number of jobs promised and more likely.

Such successful negotiations have proved rare. Most cases ended in deadlock. Inflated Aboriginal expectations induced by politicians and uncertainties of title created by the High Court resulted in an investors' strike. And without investment there can be no development.

Even BHP, capitalised at nearly $25 billion, was not big enough to ignore the crisis. Chief executive John Prescott told viewers of *Business Sunday*:

> "I'm sufficiently concerned about it to realise that we're not likely to be able to proceed in some areas. If you cannot bring a new project on line when you expect to, you lose the market opportunity and you lose it forever because someone else picks it up...And so uncertainties such as those associated with Mabo are a worry."

Nearly 80 per cent of companies surveyed for the Mining Industry Council rated themselves *"highly concerned"* about the Mabo situation, and more than half were worried that it would have a *"major effect"* on their business prospects. The Council's director, Lauchlan McIntosh, said mining companies had many projects *"on hold or about to go on hold."*

The banks were, as always, the key. First to go public was the local subsidiary of a New York powerhouse: Scott Reid, managing director of Chase Manhattan Bank Australia, said that investment plans worth several hundred million dollars, including one for at least $100 million, had been shifted onto the back burner:

> "If a project is Mabo-affected, it cannot go forward – it is as simple as that. Project finance is enormously risky in the first place. Mabo can cast a pall over the whole thing."

Alan Cullen, executive director of the Australian Bankers' Association, confirmed that both domestic and foreign banks were knocking back multi-million-dollar projects, notably in mining and tourism because *"they are the big-ticket items in the areas where Aborigines might have the biggest claim to native title."*

(Cullen later triggered a rash of telephone protests to Melbourne radio station 3AW when he quoted a hypothetical miner as saying: *"Well, if the Abos don't exercise their right of veto within a certain time, we can go ahead."* Some listeners were offended by the word Abo – part of the mind-set which we will examine in the next chapter. Cullen commented: *"I've used Abo all my life. To me it's not a derogatory word."* Nor is it to most Australians.)

Graham Campbell, Federal MP for the huge electorate of Kalgoorlie, pitched in with the fact that he knew banks had "pulled the plug" on a $10 million Kimberley project because of Mabo uncertainties.

Mounting concern united eight major industry organisations who represented, as they said, *"almost the entire private sector"* in demanding that the government enter into *"full and detailed consultation with all parties"* – consultation which *"is now seriously overdue."* They complained, with strong justification:

> "The Mabo debate is out of hand and becoming increasingly divisive. It is creating an unnecessary level of uncertainty within the business community and among overseas investors...By going it alone, the Federal Government will only end up with a position which fails to accommodate the interests of the affected parties, scares off investment and exacerbates divisions within the Australian community...It is a matter of great concern that the Federal Government is attempting to finalise legislation without adequate and on-going consultation with industry."

This considerable coalition – which included the Australian Chamber of Commerce and Industry, the Australian Mining Industry Council, the National Farmers Federation and the Business Council of Australia – spelled out six essentials in any agreement:

1. Existing property titles to be confirmed;

2. Crown ownership of mineral resources to be confirmed;

3. Any compensation to Aborigines to be paid by the Federal Government;

4. States to validate existing titles and the Commonwealth to pass complementary legislation;

5. Legal costs to landholders hit by claims on grants made before 30 June 1993 to be paid by the Government;

6. Efficient court procedures to be set up to speed resolution of claims.

Officers of the Mining Industry Council issued two warnings – one concerning the impact of the Mabo Judgment on the duties of company directors and auditors, the other on the likelihood of international investors giving Australia the flick. First, Geoffrey Ewing:

> "Corporate laws impose on company directors an obligation to report periodically on the valuation of fixed assets and investments. The Mabo decision has created a scenario where such valuations may become extraordinarily difficult. If, because of the possibility of a claim for native title, the directors cannot certify that titles are valued at a true and fair figure, then the asset backing of the company will be questioned. That will affect the valuation of the stock. Similarly, if auditors feel claims to native title are likely to be successful, or may even have a chance of being successful, they may feel that they have to qualify the directors' report."

Campbell Anderson, as president of the Council and as a prominent mining executive, was depressed by the prospects for the industry which brings such riches to Australia:

> "The Mabo decision is only one in a long series of events which have progressively reduced the areas within Australia that can be prospected for mining. Australia has undoubted geological potential, but so have other countries. It remains to be seen whether and how soon the problems of land access surpass the geological attraction. If and when this happens, I truly hope that Australia has found another way to generate wealth."

Robert Champion de Crespigny, chief executive of the big Normandy Poseidon mining conglomerate, was equally depressed by Mabo and the impact of World Heritage listings, but on slightly different grounds:

"Sovereign risk is getting more and more unsatisfactory. Internationally now, if we're ranked on sovereign risk, we're regarded as one of the countries that is least stable. There is no doubt doing business in Indonesia for mining companies is simpler, more straightforward and much less sovereign risk than in this country."

The Australian Financial Review pointed to the hidden cost of any further Mabo-induced impediments to the mining industry:

"That cost would be difficult to prove, and almost impossible to measure. It would arise in part from the mineral exploration that did *not* take place. It would be the loss of the income from the mineral deposits that were *not* discovered."

And in a role not usually attributed to brokers – that of a political commentator – Laurie Cox, chairman of the Australian Stock Exchange, put his finger on a vital point:

"Political correctness in Canberra seems to be the overriding, or even the sole valid criterion for everything…There seem to be a lot of people in Australia who are busy applauding the correctness of the Mabo Judgment. In doing so they are blind to the very serious damage being caused to investment in this country, and particularly foreign investment."

Chapter Eleven

Keating III: Debate By Abuse

Relationships with Paul Keating are simple. You either agree with him or you are a mongrel. There are any number of mongrels involved with the Mabo mess:

> **Tim Fischer:** "Crude and primitive remarks of the leader of the National Party who is obviously in a position way beyond his capacities in life."

– Keating broadside from Seoul in South Korea where his mind should have been on other things

> **Hugh Morgan:** "Technically he was wrong, historically he was wrong...That is sheer extravagance of language. It is totally untrue. It is absolutely untrue. And it is a statement not worthy of him."

– Keating commenting on the business executive's speech about the Mabo Judgment affecting property values

> **Jeff Kennett :** "Just mischievous and wrong."

– Keating responding to the Victorian Premier's statement that he had legal advice that people's backyards are at risk after the Mabo Judgment

> **Richard Court:** "His threat to hold a racially-based referendum raises his anti-Aboriginal campaign to a new and dangerous level and should be viewed with disdain by all fair-minded Australians."
>
> – *Keating's little-sir-echo, Robert Tickner*

Keating's most intense wrath seemed to be stirred up by Hugh Morgan, Western Mining's chief executive, probably because he was the first prominent businessman to sound the alarm over the Mabo Judgment, but possibly because Morgan represents everything that Keating doesn't. While both are much the same age, Morgan has Welsh blood, Keating has Irish; Morgan went to Anglican Geelong Grammar, Keating to Catholic de la Salle; Morgan has degrees in law and commerce, Keating left school at fourteen; Morgan's father had been managing director of Western Mining before him, Keating's father mended boilers.

Morgan blew the whistle on the Mabo Judgment when invited to give the Joe and Enid Lyons Memorial Lecture (Lyons was a former Prime Minister and his widow the first woman member of the House of Representatives and the first woman minister) at the Australian National University four months after the decisions were handed down.

He reviewed the abandonment of *terra nullius* and said the change, if at all, should have been made via legislation or referendum and *"not by the High Court on some social adventure of its own."* He went on: *"I believe that what has been put at risk now is the whole legal framework of property rights throughout the community."* And expecting, like almost everyone else, a change of government, he said:

> "One of the early Bills a coalition government must put to the Parliament, and if necessary to a double-dissolution election, is either repeal of, or substantial amendment to, the *Racial Discrimination Act 1975.*

"It is a melancholy but necessary consequence that the judgments of the High Court...will now become part of, indeed central to, partisan political debate in Australia."

How right he was. The very next afternoon Keating was on his feet in Parliament, putting in the boot as only he cares to do:

"What we have here is just bigotry. It is the voice of ignorance, the voice of hysteria and the voice of the nineteenth century.

"With all the prejudice, banality and venality which Mr Morgan could muster, he went on to make the claim that no title should ever have been vested in the Aboriginal people. It is a prejudiced view which is totally intolerant and should be condemned out of hand."

Morgan made Mabo into news, and it has remained so ever since. That suited his crusade against the Judgment. It certainly did not suit Keating. For – as that knowing political reporter and now editor of the *Canberra Times*, Michelle Grattan, observed as the brawls developed: *"Almost always the politics of Aboriginal affairs are no-win."*

Morgan got right up Keating's nose just three weeks after Labor's surprise win in the autumn election of 1993. Giving the keynote address to the centenary conference of the Australian Institute of Mining and Metallurgy in Adelaide, he cited a couple of Keating's speeches – the Redfern one in which he took the confessional route of *"We did the dispossessing"* etc., and his talk to staff on the eve of the election in which he said: *"I'm more convinced than ever that we've got to make peace with the Aborigines...I think we've got a tremendous opportunity with the Mabo decision to do something with Aboriginal reconciliation."* Morgan gave a strong response:

"Here is this gifted son of the New South Wales Right, who once poured so much scorn on the basket-weavers of Balmain and on the politics of the warm inner glow, now identifying completely with those he once sought to politically destroy.

"The Prime Minister wants to make peace with the Aborigines. We are not at war with the Aborigines and have never been at war with them, despite recent attempts to rewrite the history of Queensland in terms of decades of warfare.

"Aborigines are Australian citizens, neither more nor less. The Prime Minister speaks of them as aliens, requiring a peace treaty or reconciliation."

Keating's lap-dog Tickner was put up to do the howling this time: *"I am both flabbergasted and saddened at the level of apparent ignorance displayed by Mr Morgan."*

Morgan's next airing of serious Mabo misgivings – in the opening address to the annual conference of the Victorian branch of the Returned Services League (RSL) – was the most telling; it was the one which prompted Keating's *"totally untrue, absolutely untrue"* outburst quoted at the start of this chapter.

Morgan knew that he would cop more abuse, saying early in his speech that anyone *"who does not believe that Aborigines of pre-settlement times were 'noble savages'...untouched by original sin, is accused of racism, bigotry or worse, particularly under parliamentary privilege."* But he was not deterred. He stated baldly that *"because of the naive adventurism of the High Court, the economic and political future of Australia has been put at risk."*

The media reports over following days highlighted reactions to the speech rather than its substance. For that reason I quote at some length a few of the passages of particular importance:

- "We are facing what is fundamentally a political problem, not a legal one. Because Mabo is a High Court judgment, we immediately briefed benchfuls of Constitutional lawyers to give us advice. These lawyers sat down and analysed Mabo according to their time-honoured techniques of legal construction. They treated Mabo as just another High Court decision. And in doing so many of them, I believe, missed the plot. Mabo is a challenge to the legitimacy of Australia including the legitimacy of the High Court itself. It is fundamentally a political document, albeit disguised in a cloak of legal reasoning. The legal analysis is necessary but, unless it is illuminated by a political understanding, then such advice can mislead."

- "The Prime Minister and the minister assisting him on Aboriginal affairs, Mr Tickner, have taken fright at the upsurge of resentment that has developed since an understanding of the implications of Mabo began to spread through the community. The main thrust of their reassurances is that freehold title, the title under which most of us own our homes, cannot be affected by Mabo. They don't tell us that only four of the seven High Court Justices decided that. But let that pass. What is much more significant is that they don't tell us that our freehold titles will slump in value if the earning capacity of our mining, pastoral, tourist, fishing and forestry industries is wound down as a consequence of Mabo."

- "Regardless of what ministers tell us, all titles to property in Australia have been devalued as a result of Mabo. A High Court which tosses aside more than two centuries of settled law in property is a High Court whose predictability has been massively down-graded. An economy, in which many classes of important property transfers have to be tested in the High Court before they can be regarded as secure, is an economy with very grave problems indeed."

- "Mabo directly threatens the unity of Australia. It brings in a separate law for one group of Australians. It encourages Aboriginal Australians to think of themselves as separate and distinct from their fellow citizens. It promises racial tension. It guarantees economic stagnation."

Keating hurried onto next evening's *A Current Affair* to give Morgan the anticipated serve, saying – without much coherence – that if only the strong prospered economically and socially then *"God help us as a society..."*

"In other words, these wealthy people who think they can put themselves up in their places with barbed wire round their front yards – that's what they would end up with in the sort of society that Mr Morgan wants to tell us that exists."

Tickner was as put out as his master, beside himself in fact: *"We've had some outrageous scaremongering and unmitigated nonsense lately on the decision of the High Court of Australia in the Mabo case, but Mr Morgan simply takes the cake."*

One might think from the amount of abuse heaped on him that Morgan was a lone voice. Far from it. But all who shared his views and went public were castigated roundly and/or hounded.

Consider Henry Bosch: an intelligent man with degrees from the University of Sydney, Balliol College (Oxford) and the *Centre d'Etudes Industrielles* (Geneva); a capable man who filled senior executive positions with manufacturing firms in Britain, Canada and Australia; a public-spirited man who has chaired industry inquiries, served on industry bodies and for five years or more was chairman of the National Companies and Securities Commission.

In recent years Bosch, who is in his sixties, was a $20,000 a year part-time consultant to the Ministry of Administrative Services, which has little to do with Aborigines. In that role he was invited to address a Strategic Leaders Forum hosted by Telecom. He called his talk Greasing the Economic Gears and, in part, argued that national responses to such difficulties as the growing foreign debt and 10 per cent unemployment were inadequate and that *"diversionary matters"* were drawing attention away from the essential issues.

He instanced Keating's campaigns for a republic and Aboriginal reconciliation, remarking with adequate accuracy that Aborigines are *"a stone age people"* and are *"the most backward 1 per cent of the population by any objective set of achievements."*

Who would argue with that? Senator Robert Francis McMullan, minister for Administrative Services, for one.

Within hours of Bosch's comments appearing in morning newspapers the senior bureaucrat in the department was asking him to review his situation; when Bosch declined, the bureaucrat advised him to reconsider over the weekend. On the Monday, with no word from Bosch, the bureaucrat wrote asking him to resign and stating that if an answer was not received within 48 hours his contract would be terminated.

McMullin denied that Bosch was being fired for holding views which were not politically correct, but he did concede: *"The views he has expressed on Aboriginals are incompatible with the role of advising the government."*

Most of the media was mute. But not Paddy McGuinness who knows well – with another eloquent Irishman, John Philpot Curran (1750-1817) – that The Price of Liberty is Eternal Vigilance. He wrote in *The Australian* the day after Bosch went:

> "When a man of undoubted integrity, who has served the community in an important government-appointed position, is unceremoniously pushed out of consultative positions because the government does not like his opinions, and denies him the right to express them, how much liberty is left to the rest of us?"

Bosch himself had the last word for the time being, in a signed article in *The Weekend Australian:*

> "It seems to be held that as long as opinions are politically correct they must be defended at all costs, but that if they are incorrect they must not be voiced. If they are (voiced) they will be derided as reactionary, racist, fascist, or some other term of unthinking abuse that substitutes for reasoned argument."

Three times in just six months Keating, Tickner *et al* were frenzied by Tim Fischer, the leader of the National Party. In any debate about national objectives, the man in the broad-brimmed hat has impeccable credentials. Raised on a Riverina grazing property at Boree Creek he was taught by the Jesuits at Xavier College in Melbourne; commissioned in the Army and served two years with the Royal Australian Regiment in Vietnam. He was a member of parliament for more than twenty years, first in Sydney and then Canberra.

He entered the Mabo debate in the summer of 1993, declaring during a radio interview in Perth that he had no time for the *"guilt industry which says that we whites must apologise for being here for two hundred years, for developing the country, for providing heaps of taxpayers' money"* to Aboriginal organisations and causes. Indeed he said he would *"take on and fight the guilt industry all the way."* This was fed overnight by the government's monitoring service to Keating's holiday home and he put out a response accusing Fischer of trying to incite *"fear and resentment"* in what he labelled a *"slur on the decent concern... and goodwill of the vast majority of Australians."* Ho-hum.

Fischer struck again at the Nationals' New South Wales conference at Wagga Wagga. This time a passing remark – that before white settlement Aborigines had not developed *"even a wheeled cart"* – was featured in the media and, once again, the real message largely passed over:

> "I would make the point, rightly or wrongly, dispossession of Aboriginal civilisation *(He should have said 'culture'; they were not, by definition, civilised – Author)* was always going to happen. Those in the guilt industry have to consider that developing cultures and people will always overtake relatively stationary cultures. All that I am saying is these things are relative and the horrors of the past were not caused by this generation of Australians."

This time Keating called on Dr Hewson, leader of the opposition, to *"put down the crude and primitive remarks of the leader of the National Party,"* but Hewson said Fischer had *"every right to raise issues that are of importance to his constituency."*

He exercised that right again just a month later at the Nationals' Queensland state conference, saying that Aborigines were not the only ones to have affinity with the land:

> "There are families in Australia who have held their land for generations. Their forebears worked the land and were buried in the land...For these farmers, their holding of land and their attachment to it is deeper than just an investment. They consider themselves custodians of the land, not merely investors in it...It is relevant to recognise that there is attachment by a lot of Australians to their land – be they black, white or otherwise."

Keating erred in his response, accusing Fischer falsely: *"He tells the people that they will lose their backyards."* A few hours later his office was obliged to back away; a spokesman said the PM's statement was meant to be *"illustrative"* only!

Richard Court, the Premier of Western Australia, who called for a referendum on Mabo; Jeff Kennett, the

Premier of Victoria, who went ahead with his own legislation to secure land titles; and Marshall Perron, chief minister of the Northern Territory, who told a press conference that Europeans had not been able to do anything to improve Aborigines' "appalling hygiene", all came in for a Commonwealth caning.

Tickner said Court's referendum would be *"blatantly discriminatory against Aboriginal people"* and reported him to the Human Rights and Equal Opportunity Commission; he said Kennett is *"the blustering clown of the Liberal Establishment"*, and he scorned Perron's comments as *"an arrogant manifestation of purported cultural superiority."*

All this was a bit too much for Colin Howard, for more than twenty years the Hearn Professor of Law at the University of Melbourne and now in private practice – a man of the highest standing. He took Tickner up on his allegation that Court's referendum would be discriminatory and a few other things beside:

> "If Mr Tickner seriously thinks that that should offend all fair-minded Australians, be unconstitutional and a breach of our international obligations, not to mention a ground for dragging a state Premier before a Commonwealth tribunal to be chastised, he needs a Disprin and a spell in a home for the bewildered."

Absolutely. But amidst all the silly slanging, something sinister was building up: the acceptance by the entire chattering classes of Keating's law that if you don't agree with us you are a mongrel. It was encapsulated by the classes' Gillian Cowlishaw – lecturer in anthropology at the University of Sydney and author of books and articles on Aborigines – in her attack on Blainey and Morgan. First note that *The Concise Oxford Dictionary* defines 'racism' as a "theory that human abilities, etc. are determined by race." Cowlishaw put a different spin on it:

> "It is, I would argue, a certain form of racism that allows these otherwise rational men to regard

the Mabo decision, which delivers limited and circumscribed rights to land previously unwanted by anyone else, as a threat to the nation."

Protests were depressingly few. McGuinness, of course: *"What we are witnessing is a climate of attempted intimidation."* John Hewson: *"Anyone who dares to disagree with Mr Keating is 'a spoiler' or 'a bigot' or 'peddling lies'."* John Howard: *"Its ruthless smearing of any Australians who dare to dissent from what the government regards as morally acceptable on Mabo confirms a deep authoritarian streak."* Richard Court: *"We have entered a dangerous age in Australia when freedom of thought is branded as racist, inflammatory, an infringement of human rights."* And the splendid Les Carlyon, writing in *Business Review Weekly:*

> "One of the worst things about modern Australia is that anyone who questions the politically correct agenda is immediately proscribed... anyone who questions the wisdom of Keating's Mabo scheme is apparently a racist."

To be sure, other forces were unleashed by the Mabo debate, too. Irene Moss, the Commonwealth's Race Discrimination Commissioner, told a conference for indigenous people that supporters of the Mabo Judgment had been subjected to *"low-level terrorism"* including hate mail. Bill Belling, of the Aboriginal Legal Service, told a Victorian government committee that *"our kids and our people have been made to suffer in the aftermath of Mabo – physical attacks have been happening in schools and streets."* Bonita Mabo, Eddie's widow, complained that her fourteen-year-old grandson had been upset by an abusive phone call to her home. Charles Perkins described a horror drive as he, his wife and their baby granddaughter – with an Aboriginal-flag sticker on the back of the car – were harassed leaving Newcastle by a hoon in a utility truck who ran them off the road. A gang of five white drunks taunted and bashed the teenage son and foster-son of activist Gary

Foley outside a Melbourne suburban pub. And the vandalism of Attorney-General Lavarch's Brisbane office and the abuse of his staff was said to be the work of thugs opposed to land rights.

As forecast, the decisions of the Mabo Six and Keating's insistence on broadening those decisions into his version of a black-white entente were dividing the people rather than uniting them. And it was set to get worse.

Chapter Twelve

Keating IV: A Different Dreamtime

"Anti-Mabo sentiment was given its head largely because pro-Mabo campaigners, including the Prime Minister, Mr Keating, raised expectations too high by linking the judgment to wider issues of reconciliation."

– The Australian, 31 July, 1993

After the ignominious fiasco of his meeting with the Premiers in Melbourne, Keating was obliged to go back to the beginning. He realised that he should make some effort to inform and shape public opinion to his reconciliation crusade. But it was fairly half-hearted. He did spend more than an hour doing talk-back with his mate John Laws on radio 2UE. He started in explaining mode:

"If Mabo meant that a claim over Circular Quay in Sydney had any strength about it, then people would have genuine concerns about their rights to interest in land and their wealth. But this decision applies only to those places where a title has not been issued and only if there's been continuous association (by Aborigines).

"I can see people thinking that in some way Aboriginal people have been treated in a preferential way. But that is not true. (Before Mabo) what was given to Aborigines included limited land opportunities and social justice in education and health...and also, in some cases, income support because often, where Aboriginal people live, there aren't the opportunities for employment."

But soon explaining gave way to anger with his callers:

"I'm not here basically to soak up all your prejudices...That's what you are really talking. You don't want to see Aboriginal Australians have any right to the land."

And to a man who phoned and said "I am not a racist", he shot back: "That is what they all say."
Next he wrote to the Premiers to tell them that he would bring in Commonwealth legislation to implement the High Court's decisions, and warning that any move to *"go it alone"* would be against the national interest. In the letter he hedged his all-or-nothing stance of their earlier meeting, saying that the *"wider Mabo issues"* of reconciliation between blacks and whites would be tackled separately.
Soon he was on his way to visit Korea and China, but the problem travelled with him; a Mabo file was prominent among his papers. We have from the *Sydney Morning Herald's* Alan Ramsey some interesting Keating observations at that time. It is quite usual for travelling Prime Ministers to ask a few reporters to come up front in the airplane for a drink and a chat. Keating invited seven of them during the three-hour flight from Seoul to Beijing. It is also a convention on those occasions that the host's words are not for quotation. But there are ways in these matters and Ramsey was just the man to know them. Thus we read:

"Paul Keating thinks Jeff Kennett is a mug liar and a bonehead. He thinks Queensland's Wayne Goss isn't a lot better. He thinks New South Wales' John Fahey and the Northern Territory's Marshall Perron are the only two state and territory leaders with any real courage in facing up to the Mabo issue. And he is determined to show the others that if this *'bath water gets too hot'* over Mabo, he'll be *'the last out'* of the tub."

He returned at the start of the new financial year and a number of onlookers thought it a fitting moment to assess his performance during the three-and-a-half months since the election. Graham Little, who teaches political psychology at the University of Melbourne, compared Keating Mark I (before the election) and Keating Mark II (post election):

"The meeting with the Premiers over Mabo and the belated discovery that talk-back callers aren't as enamoured with reform are reminders that, however desirable and necessary the push for change is, it needs to be accompanied by plenty of the political nous we associate with Keating Mark I."

Geoffrey Barker, who took over from Michelle Grattan as *The Age's* chief political correspondent, was a little tougher:

"He has run into trouble, not because he is wrong on Mabo or the republic, but because of brashness...A creature of conflict, the Prime Minister has made little serious effort to seek and build a national consensus on either issue. His natural stance is as a warrior, not the healer; and it has showed."

Glenn Milne, who is billed as the Political Editor of *The Australian*, was harshest of all:

> "Aboriginal reconciliation is his major preoccupation...Keating's behaviour was driven by righteousness and he foundered on his own moral certainty, paying the price for his own glorious isolation...The almost overwhelming opinion within government is that Mabo is now an unholy mess, with Keating culpable for vacating the field to the venality of the talk-back radio hosts and the far right."

There was one voice in marked contrast; talking of policy based on *"both the heart and the head"* it came up with glowing report:

> "In eighteen months (as PM) Keating changed the language of Australian politics, boosted spending on public infrastructure, put a republic on the agenda, boosted Aboriginal reconciliation, turned Australia's attention to the Asia-Pacific, put together a national training authority with the states – and won an election."

Who was the author? Why, Don Russell. And who is Russell? Keating's closest adviser for years, recently rewarded by being posted as His Excellency the Australian Ambassador in Washington. Ho-hum again.

The bureaucrats who by then had been working for a year on the government response to the Mabo Judgment kept on slugging, talking to their opposite numbers in each State and meeting again with selected Aboriginal leaders. The latest drafting notes for legislation displeased the Aborigines because their right to veto mining projects on native-title land was being watered down. Rob Riley, of the Western Australian Aboriginal Legal Service, accused the government of giving in to pressure from the mining and pastoral industries. Sol Bellear, acting chairman of ATSIC, said *"social justice measures"* must be written into any legislation. And in a twist on the old anti-British cry of *'no taxation without representation'* he insisted on *"no validation without compensation."*

Other pressures were coming onto Keating. Cheryl Kernot – leader of the Democrats who, after the change-over on 1 July, still held the balance of power in the Senate – told him during an hour-long tête-a-tête that they, too, wanted to see a complete social package for Aborigines in the legislation. Rick Farley of the National Farmers Federation was insisting that leasehold pastoral properties must be protected from native-title claims.

And even friends were stoking it up: a conference of the national Left of the Labor Party resolved that, under the legislation, Aborigines *"must be involved, particularly in negotiations relating to mining projects where it can be demonstrated they still have an interest"*. Senator Margaret Reynolds, a teacher from Townsville and convener of the Left's Mabo campaign committee, sent word to Keating: *"Don't let those manipulative people from behind the scenes push you off track – be very, very genuine."* And Barry Jones, in his role as president of the Labor Party, told Keating via ABC radio that he *"had to get the Premiers back inside the tent"* because the *"ownership of land and the right to land is essentially a State power."* He advised:

> "Unless you get agreement from the States, the Commonwealth is simply using its pre-emptive power under the Constitution, and that might prove to be completely inappropriate."

As the bureaucrats toiled on, a proposition turning all previous thinking on its head was thrown into the ring by just-arrived-consultant Phillip Toyne and his legal mate and Weipa protaganist, Castan QC. It was that ALL vacant Crown land be recognised as native-title land. This would reverse the need for Aboriginal groups to claim the land and prove their on-going connection with it and put the onus on State governments – acting on behalf of miners or tourist developers or whoever – to seek approval from a tribunal (and implicitly from the Aboriginal titleholders) to go ahead. It was a projection of the lateral thinking Gastan put into his landmark claim for the Wik peoples.

But another climax was building. The bureaucrats, after three weeks of constant rewriting, had done their best and Cabinet members settled to a weekend of reading. Jeff Kennett had already introduced his go-it-alone legislation to validate titles in Victoria, and that weekend the Western Australian Liberal Party conference voted four-to-one in favour of Court's push for a national referendum on Mabo.

Most people said the Cabinet meeting which reached views, as Keating described them afterwards, *"on what could amount to baselines for Commonwealth legislation"* lasted six hours; Keating said seven. Either way it was a knock-down, drag-out affair. Left-wing members, including Deputy Prime Minister Brian Howe and Aboriginal Affairs Minister Tickner, caucused beforehand and resolved to make sure that Aboriginals would have a right of veto over developments on their land. Keating, on the other hand, had assured the Premiers at the abortive meeting in June that there would be no native-title veto. So the battle lines were drawn.

In the dog's breakfast that eventually emerged, neither side won. Instead it was decided that wherever Aborigines are the holders of native title they have a *"right of negotiation"* with any developers. Then, if those negotiations failed to find agreement inside, say, three months, the matter would be put before either a State or Commonwealth tribunal. And after that either the State or the Commonwealth could override the tribunal *"in the national interest."* If you want to see just what a mess it would lead to, heed the verbatim words Keating used the following evening on SBS's *Dateline* program:

> "The Commonwealth tribunal can override a State tribunal – we need and will get State legislation... If there isn't a satisfactory State attitude, and legislation that is satisfactory to the Commonwealth, then the Commonwealth tribunal would operate in the States where the Commonwealth is designated to operate...If a State brings

its policy up to the standard of the Commonwealth, their tribunal would operate and, therefore, their government would have the right to override the decision of the tribunal."

It would have been funny if it was not so awful. And the uncertainty which baffled everyone was not helped next day by Frank Walker, the Special Minister of State, who made this howler: *"It would take me a week to explain it succinctly."*

But Cabinet decided upon an even greater iniquity: they agreed that while native title would be extinguished for all time by residential, pastoral and tourist leases, it would be **revived when a mining lease expired** and the miners, if they wished to go on working the site, would have to renegotiate with the Aborigines. Some leaseholders, as George Orwell might have said, would be more equal than others.

It has been a scandalous characteristic of all recent relations with or about Aborigines – including the High Court's decisions – that some Australians have better rights than others; usually it favoured the Aborigines themselves, but Cabinet's latest plan elevated graziers and hoteliers above miners, despite the vital fact that miners bring in the greatest amount of export earnings.

There were, not unexpectedly and absolutely justifiably, strong protests by the mining industry and by the States. Kennett said the proposals were a *"sham"* and *"obviously discriminate against the mining industry and will not stand the test of law,"* and Court said: *"Under the Constitution, States have full responsibility for land-administration issues and for the granting of land titles – these proposals see the Federal Government taking over a lot of that and we oppose them."*

For once the coalition parties formulated a response; their sub-committe on Mabo, after a long meeting in Sydney, issued a paper which said, in part:

> "Existing mineral rights under State and Territory laws should be protected and existing access by industry to minerals should remain. The

Coalition accepts that the High Court has determined that native title exists. However, up to this point in time, native title has only been proven in relation to the Murray Islands. Whether, how, where, and in what form it will translate in other circumstances is, as yet, unspecified and undetermined."

Thank goodness the paper also said: *"Any resolution of the issues raised by the Mabo case should proceed on the basis that all Australians should be treated equally under the law."*

What did the Aborigines think of Cabinet's proposals? For the first time, there was a chance that there might be an answer on which some credence could be placed – because something unique was about to unfold.

It is quite wrong to think of Aborigines as one people with a set of common beliefs and attitudes. There are more than five hundred clans or communities and as many points of view. That is one reason why it is so difficult to reach negotiated agreements. And we saw earlier that if one set of leaders – like those who met with Keating and his colleagues back in April – is selected, others criticise them and say they have no right to speak on behalf of any group but their own.

The more worldly-wise Aborigines acknowledge the situation, and some of them sought to overcome it in the closing stages of the Mabo debate. Initiated by three prominent Jawoyn Aborigines – the brothers Dodson (Pat of the flowing beard, who is chairman of the Council for Aboriginal Reconciliation, and the younger and clean-shaven Mick, who is the Commissioner for Aboriginal Social Justice, plus John Ah Kit of the Jawoyn Association and the Northern Land Council) – word went out to tribes and clans all over the country, calling leaders to the first-ever widely-representative discussion of affairs. Never before in literally thousands of years had such a gathering been summoned!

The meeting was called for the week following Cabinet's long debate. The immediate purpose was to examine the legislative proposals. But, as Pat Dodson explained: *"It's not a one-off occasion. This will be followed up, and there will be more and more discussions and debate within Aboriginal circles."*

The location was called Manyallaluk, a pleasant grassy stretch below the old homestead on Eva Valley station, owned by the Jawoyn, near the Katherine Gorge in the Northern Territory; John Ah Kit called it *"a beautiful, peaceful place, full of significance."*

Between four and five hundred, many of them women, arrived carrying their bedrolls and ready to sleep under the stars. Eighty had their air fares paid, but the majority travelled by car, some for thousands of kilometres. They drove in past a sign announcing *"You are now entering Aboriginal-controlled land"* and another warning that alcohol and drugs were banned. Reporters were banned, too, and armed patrolmen made the ban stick.

For three days they talked, and word filtered out that the denial of a veto by native titleholders was the big issue; representatives of the Aboriginal Legal Services demanded that all the Aboriginals on the Reconciliation Council resign in a block protest, but tribal elders came out strongly in support of reconciliation.

At five o'clock on the third afternoon the media were allowed in to receive the 600-word Eva Valley Statement and attend an open-air press conference.

The Statement was totally bad news for Paul Keating, the white man who, more than any other, champions their cause. It spelled out five principles which it said the government must act upon:

1. Aboriginal rights must be recognised and protected.

2. Aboriginal land titles *"cannot be extinguished by grants of any interest."*

3. No grants can be made "without the informed consent of all relevant titleholders" – the veto.

4. Aboriginal title to be declared on reserves and other "defined lands" – probably National Parks.

5. Absolute Aboriginal authority over sacred sites.

Three of the men chosen to take the Statement to Keating gave him a blast up front:

Mick Dodson: "We don't agree with anything they've done. They haven't bothered to talk to us about it. They haven't negotiated with us about it. And they don't have our consent to do what they want to do...Whatever happens on our land must be a matter for us and us alone."

Galarrwuy Yunupingu (chairman of Northern Land Council and a member of the Council for Reconciliation): "The Prime Minister has backed off his commitment to Aboriginal people...By going ahead and proposing the legislation he has undermined the work the Council has done so far. He felt the pressure from the land developers that Mabo is a threat to the country."

Michael Mansell (of the self-styled Aboriginal Provisional Government): "We're saying leave us alone. Let us get on with our own lives on our own land. Give us some form of protection so we can bring up our kids on our land without other people telling us what to do."

Keating's first response was anger. In a pavement grab for the television reporters he, to all intents and purposes, called the Aborigines liars:

"The claim yesterday by the Aboriginal community was that the government hasn't consulted them. That was patently untrue. The full Cabinet met with about thirty broad representatives from the Aboriginal community; then a smaller representative group met with the ministerial committee, and I've seen Mr Dodson on three occasions, all for about an hour each, and I saw representatives of the Land Councils for about an hour before the last Cabinet meeting."

A frustrated Keating found himself under seige. It was not only the Aborigines who were jacking up on him. So were the States. And so was the mining industry.

Then, early in Spring 1993, when he did release his virtually-unchanged legislative proposals for public discussion, the seige was intensified. He was in a frightful mess – most of it of his own making.

Chapter Thirteen

No Work Back O' Bourke

Bourke is 781 kilometres up the Mitchell Highway north-west of Sydney and the most remote major town in New South Wales. Henry Lawson lived there a hundred years ago, in the Carriers' Arms, and hated it...

> "On glaring iron-roofs of Bourke, the scorching,
>   blinding sandstorms blew,
> And there was nothing beautiful in Ninety-one
>   and Ninety-two."

These days most of Bourke is much better. There are actually two Bourkes. On the eastern bank of the Darling River is a spruce sort of place with some good buildings – the old administrative headquarters has walls of corrugated iron unusually attached horizontally under a splendid widely-overhanging roof; most houses are freshly painted and gardens trim; people smile even when the district is in drought, which is most of the time.

The other Bourke is on the western bank. Go across there – it is unwise to go on foot and certainly not after dark – and the prospect is barely believable. Not one window unbroken, hardly a door still hanging; rusty sheets of iron the only protection against the dust storms. These semi-derelict streets are home to the descendants of the Ngyammba and Wangkumara. And they are so depressing.

Drive nearly 350 kilometres south-west beside the Darling and, crossing the magnificent cast-iron bridge which used to lift to let the steamers through, you are in Wilcannia, which also has some fine old buildings, this time in sandstone. If it is pension day, the intersection of the town's two shopping streets presents a scene of Hogarthian horror. On the pavements of all four corners people, many of them women, are sprawled in stupor; but for a few men trying to punch each other in slow motion, one could think a mighty blast had struck.

The latest census shows that two-thirds of all Aborigines live in "urban centres" – cities and towns of more than one thousand inhabitants. Given that there are now 257,333 people who call themselves Aborigines, that means a maximum of some 85,000 – less than half of one per cent of the whole population – live in tribal possession of lands which they might be able to claim under the Mabo Judgment.

(The Aboriginal population has had a remarkable increase during the Whitlam-Hawke-Keating years of inflated expectations; when Whitlam won power there were only 115,953, today there are more than twice that number. The definition of who is an Aborigine is in *A Review of the Administration of the Working Definition of Aboriginal and Torres Strait Islanders* put out by the Department of Aboriginal Affairs in 1981, and is a prime example of bureaucratic circularity:

> "An Aboriginal or Torres Strait Islander is a person of Aboriginal or Torres Strait Islander descent who identifies as an Aboriginal or Torres Strait Islander and is accepted as such by the community in which he lives."

Ron Brunton, in his *Black Suffering, White Guilt?*, says many people are asserting *"Aboriginal identity which they had previously denied"* and speculates that there may be some people seeking *"to take advantage of special benefits available only to Aborigines"* – benefits which B.A. Santamaria estimates to have been at least $25 billion since the Whitlam days.)

It is surely remarkable that the Mabo crisis – and it is a national crisis of considerable proportions – revolves round the 0.48 per cent of the population which already owns 15 per cent of the whole continent – albeit much of it poor country – and has designs on a great deal more.

This suggests that some attention must be paid to those who believe that Mabo is part of a wider agenda – the drive for a separate sovereign state.

The self-styled Aboriginal Provisional Government, of which Mansell is the secretary, said in an article headed "Towards Aboriginal Sovereignty" in a publication of Friends of the Earth in July 1990:

> "Let it be clearly understood that the Aboriginal Provisional Government wants an Aboriginal State to be established with all the control vested back to the Aboriginal communities...The residual powers of negotiation with foreign governments to be vested in Aboriginal Provisional Government."

(Mansell and his mates were often referred to by the main bodies of Aborigines as the ratbags of the Aboriginal Industry; even to the chattering classes their ideas were considered too way out. But Mansell was one of the first chosen at the Eva Valley gathering to negotiate with Keating on behalf of Aborigines.)

As recently as April 1993 a newspaper headline, "New Nation Tipped for 2000", covered a talk by associate professor Henry Reynolds, an accepted authority on Aboriginal matters, at James Cook University in which he was reported to have said that Mabo *"added momentum to the Aboriginal nationalist movement"* and that *"Aborigines will achieve a nation state by the year 2000."*

A man who is particularly concerned by this possibility is the lawyer and former State minister William Hassell, currently president of the Liberal Party in Western Australia. He told a Mabo conference of the Samuel Griffith Society in Melbourne:

> "Put very simply, the wider agenda is to create an Aboriginal, separate, sovereign state, geographically within Australia, but only tenuously a part of the Australian nation...Mabo supports the separateness of Aboriginal people and their special rights and privileges."

(Ruling out any idea of the High Court being *"a party to the fulfilment of the Aboriginal national agenda,"* Hassel turned the usual racist gibes by saying that the Mabo Judgment was, in fact, racist:

> "Mabo creates privilege – legal privilege based on race. No Australian who is not an Aboriginal person or a Torres Strait Islander is eligible to make any claim for native title.")

A wider agenda or not, the Mabo Judgment has certainly been divisive and destructive. And it has probably done nobody, white or black, any good – except, of course, the lawyers who always win. Charles Perkins, the first Aboriginal university graduate (BA Sydney) and long a public figure, told a health conference in Darwin during the winter of 1993 that Aboriginal peoples are more divided, disorganised and captive than ever before:

> "We fight like hungry black dogs over a diminishing budgetary bone thrown to us by our white and black manipulators."

Selected Bibliography

d'Alpuget, Blanche *Robert J. Hawke* Melbourne 1984

Anson, Stan *Hawke: An emotional life* Melbourne 1992

Beckett, Jeremy (ed) *Past and Present: The Construction of Aboriginality* Sydney 1988

Blainey, Geoffrey *The Rush that Never Ended* Melbourne 1963; *Triumph of the Nomads* Melbourne 1975

Brunton, Ron *Black Suffering, White Guilt?* Melbourne 1993

Carew, Edna *Paul Keating Prime Minister* Sydney 1992

Clark, CMH *A History of Australia* Vols 1 to 6 Melbourne 1962 – 87

Coombs, HC *Trial Balance* Melbourne 1981

Crawford, RM *Australia* Melbourne 1974

Durack, Peter; Brunton, Ron & Rutherford, Tony *Mabo and After* Melbourne 1993

Flinders, Matthew *A Voyage to Terra Australis* London 1814

Goody, Jack *The Domestication of the Savage Mind* Cambridge 1977

Gordon, Michael *A Question of Leadership* Brisbane 1993

Horne, Donald *The Lucky Country* Melbourne 1964

Hughes, Robert *The Fatal Shore* London 1987

Idriess, Ion L *Drums of Mer* Sydney 1933

Jennett, Christine *Hawke and Australian Public Policy* Melbourne 1990

Kelly, Paul *The Hawke Ascendancy* Sydney 1984; *The End of Certainty* Sydney 1992

McGregor, Craig *Profile of Australia* London 1966

Menzies, Sir Robert *The Measure of the Years* Melbourne 1970

Nairn, Bede *The Big Fella* Melbourne 1986

Oakes, Laurie and Solomon, David *The Making of an Australian Prime Minister* Melbourne 1973

Reid, Alan *The Whitlam Venture* Melbourne 1976

Reynolds, Henry *The Other Side of the Frontier* Melbourne 1982

Rivett, Rohan *Australia* London 1968

Ryan, Lyndall *Aborigines and Islanders* in *From Fraser to Hawke* Melbourne 1989

Sharp, Nonie *A Landmark: The Murray Island Case* in *Arena* (No. 94) Melbourne 1991

Souter, Gavin *Acts of Parliament* Melbourne 1988

Strehlow, TGH *Aranda Traditions* Melbourne 1947; *Journey to Horseshoe Bend* Melbourne 1969

Wallace, AR *The Geographic Distribution of Animals* London 1876

Whitlam, Gough *The Whitlam Government 1972 – 1975* Melbourne 1985

Index

A

Abeles, Peter 45
Aboriginal
  assimilation 24
  claims 5-6, 92-102
  embassy 2, 41
  land councils 34, 36, 42, 80, 96
  land rights 2, 20, 22, 25, 28, 29, 34, 36, 39, 40, 71, 75, 82, 125
  mining veto 34, 39, 40, 85, 96, 124, 126, 129
  origins and early years 15-26
  possessions and welfare 12, 33, 37, 54, 95
  reconciliation 4, 5, 46, 53, 77, 79, 82, 111, 115, 122
  self government/ sovereignty 13-14, 80, 135-136
  treaty 3, 12, 42, 44, 135
Aboriginal Affairs, Ministry for 29, 33, 39, 44
Aboriginal and Torres Strait Islander Commission (ATSIC) 43-44, 79, 80, 99
Aboriginal Industry 5, 8, 54

Aboriginal Land Fund 29, 37
Aboriginal Land Rights (Northern Territory) Act 1976 36, 95
Aboriginal Legal Service 5, 33, 43, 54, 95, 100, 102, 119, 124
Aboriginal Provisional Government 13, 93, 130, 135
Adams, Phillip 8
The Age 3, 12, 104, 123
Ah Kit, John 103-104, 128
d'Alpuget, Blanche 38
Anderson, Campbell 95, 107
Anna Creek 93
Anson, Stan 38, 46
Arabunna People 93
Aranda People 18, 96
Arena Marxist Journal 59
Arnhem Land 28
Arnold, Lynn 86
Asia Pacific Economic Co-Operation (APEC) 77
Aurukun 97-98
The Australian 9, 27, 70, 91, 115, 121, 123
Australian Bankers' Association 105

Australian Chamber of Commerce and Industry 79, 106
Australian Financial Review 10, 86, 108
Australian Lawyer 74, 76
Australian Mining Industry Council 11, 79, 86, 96, 97, 105, 106
Australian National Opinion Polls (ANOP) 40
Australian Security Intelligence Organisation (ASIO) 30
Australian Stock Exchange (ASX) 108

B

Bankstown 49
Barker, Geoffrey 123
Barker, Ian 97
Barmah State Forest 5, 92
Barnard, Lance 30
Barton, Edmund 66
Barunga 44, 47
Baume, Peter 37
Bauxite 82, 97-98
Beazley, kim 47
Bell, Duncan 5
Bellear, Sol 124
Belling, Bill 119
BHP 11, 46-47, 94, 104
Bicentenary 44
Bidjara People 6, 100
Birdsell, Joseph 16
Bjelke-Petersen, Johannes 60
Blackburn, Richard 28, 58
Black Community School 57
Blackshield, Tony 62
Blainey, Geoffrey 7, 13, 16, 22, 99, 118
Borroloola 83
Bosch, Henry 114-115

Bourke 133
Breadon, Bruce 80
Brennan, Francis Gerard 67, 71
Brennan, Frank 80, 86
Brisbane CBD 5, 100
Brooks, Freddie 21
Brunton, Ron 43, 61, 134
Bryant, Gordon 30-32
Burke, Brian 39-40, 95
Burton, Tom 86
Burton, William 20
Burunga People 95
Business Council of Australia 11, 79, 106
Business Review Weekly 6, 119
Bustard, H.R. 31

C

Campbell, Graeme 76, 105
Canberra 5, 102
Cape York Land Council 80
Cape York Peninsula 6, 97-100
Carew, Edna 51
Carlyon, Les 6, 119
Carnarvon Range 6, 100
Carpentarians 17
Castan, Aaron Ronald 60, 81, 92, 97-99, 125
Cavanagh, James 33-34
Central Land Council 80, 96
Century Project 100
Champion, Malcolm 93
Champion de Crespigne, Robert 107
Chaney, Fred 37, 41
Charles (Prince) 44
Chase Manhattan Bank Australia 105
Chattering Classes 7-9, 12, 24, 118
Chifley, Ben 8, 27

Chubb, Philip 47
Clark, Geoff 88
Clark, Manning 16, 19, 21, 51, 66
Cleary, Phil 75
Coalition 127-128
Coe, Paul 101
Collins, Robert 47
Comalco 98-100
Communist Party of Australia 59
Connolly, Peter 74
Constitution of the Commonwealth of Australia 24, 25, 35, 60, 62
Convicts 19, 20
Cook, James 18, 61
Coombs, Herbert Cole 2, 25, 31-32, 41, 45, 58
Coronation Hill 46-47
Council for Aboriginal Affairs 25, 30, 32
Council for Aboriginal Reconciliation Act 1991 46
Council of Australian Governments (COAG) 84-89
Court, Richard 86-89, 94, 110, 117, 119, 127
Cowlishaw, Gillian 118
Cox, Laurie 108
CRA 94, 99-100
Crean, Simon 78
Cross, Manfred 30
Cullen, Alan 105
Curtin, John 27

D

Dauar Island 58
Davies, Rob 10
Dawkins, John 78, 87
Dawson, Daryl Michael 67, 71
Deakin, Alfred 66

Deane, William Patrick 67, 71
Dexter, Barrie 31-32
Dieri Association 93
Dixon, Owen 68-69
Dodson, Michael 81, 86, 128, 130
Dodson, Patrick 42, 80, 128
Droop, Paul 10
Drums of Mer 59

E

Ellery, Peter 94
Ernst and Young 10
Eva Valley 104, 129, 135
Evans, Harold 98
Ewing, Geoffrey 86, 97, 107
External Affairs Powers 35

F

Fahey, John 86, 123
Farley, Rick 86, 125
Farmer, Richard 53
Finnis Springs 93
Fischer, Tim 109, 116-117
Flanagan, Martin 12
Flinders Island 92
Flinders, Matthew 59, 98
Foley, Gary 119
Franklin River 36
Franks, Arnold 8
Fraser Island 5, 101
Fraser, Malcolm 36-38, 41

G

Galligan, Brian 69
Game, Philip 50
Gaudron, Mary Genevieve 68, 71
George, Jean 80
Georges, George 31-32
Geelong Advertiser 21
Gorton, John 25
Goss, Wayne 86, 99, 123

Gove Peninsula 28, 30, 58
Graham, Mary 80
Grasby, Al 58
Grattan, Michelle 111
Greenwood, Ivor 35
Griffith, Samuel 66
Groom, Ray 86
Gungalidda People 100
Gurindji People 2

H

Hand, Gerry, 42, 44
Hand, Maree 44
Hasluck, Paul 30
Hassell, William 135-136
Hawke, Hazel 44
Hawke, Stephen 38
Hawke, Robert James Lee 3, 12, 37-47
Hewson, John 117, 118
High Court of Australia 1, 5, 7, 28, 35, 59-60, 62-63, 65-76, 87, 110-113, 128, 136
Hocking, Barbara 58, 60
Holding, Clyde 39, 42
Hollings, Les 9
Hollway, Sandy 78
Holt, Harold 25
Horne, Donald 24
Howard, Colin 74, 118
Howard, John 45, 118
Howe, Brian 126
Hughes, Robert 16, 18

I

Idriess, Ion L. 59
Indonesia 15
International Convention on the Elimination of all Forms of Racial Discrimination 34
Investors 9-12, 79, 83, 87, 103-108
Iora People 19

J

James Capel & Co 10
James Cook University 58, 59, 135
Jawoyn People 47, 103-104, 128
Johnson, Leslie 33
Jones, Barry 125

K

Kaiser Aluminium 98
Kakadu National Park 46
Katherine Gorge 103, 129
Keating, Annita 53
Keating, Matt and Min 49, 110
Keating, Paul John
    abuse 10, 51, 109-120
    background 49-51
    Prime Minister 49-55, 77-90, 121-131
    reconciliation 4, 5, 53, 77, 82, 111, 115, 122
    Redfern speech 4, 54-55, 77-78, 111
    republican drive 12, 53, 77, 115
    Treasurer 45-47, 51
Kelly, Ned 61
Kelly, Paul 51
Kelly, Roslyn 41
Kelty, Bill 45
Kennett, Jeffrey 73, 86-89, 109, 117, 123, 126, 127
Keon-Cohen, Bryan 60, 92
Kernot, Cheryl 125
Kerr, John 36
Kiddle, Margaret Loch 21
Killoran, Patrick 63
Kimberley Land Council 80, 95
Kimberley Plateau 37

Index

Kirribilli House 45
Kosciusko National Park 5, 102
Kurdanji People 82

L

Lang, J.T. 49-51
Las 58
Lavarch, Michael 70, 78, 119
Lawrence, Carmen 95
Laws, John 121
Lawson, Henry 50, 133
Lee, Michael 78
Lehman Brothers International 10
Little, Graham 123
Lodge (The) 53
Lyons, Joe and Enid 110
Lyons (solicitors) 97-99

M

McArthur River 82-84
McGregor, Craig 24
McGuinness, Padraic P. 70, 73, 115, 118
McMahon, William 2, 26
McMullan, Robert 115
MacPherson, Jane 96
McLachlan, Ian 7
McIntosh, Lauchlan 74, 105
McIntyre, Greg 58, 60, 73
McHugh, Michael Hudson 68, 71
Mabo, Boneta 57, 119
Mabo, Eddie 57-63
Mabo v Queensland 5, 6, 12, 59-60, 62-63, 70-74, 113
Makarrata 41, 42
Malo 58-59, 63
Mannalargenna 92
Manne, Robert 53
Mansell, Michael 93, 130, 135

Maoris 22, 82
Marcus, Julie 3
Marubeni 83
Mason, Anthony Frank 66, 69-70, 74-76
Mawby, Maurice 98
Menzies, Robert Gordon 25, 68, 69
Mer Island 57-63
Meriams 58, 60
Midena, Brett 83
Miles, Chris 45
Milirrpum v Nabalco 28
Milne, Glenn 123
MIM Holdings 82
Mitsubishi Materials 83
Mitsui 10, 83
Monden, Tsutomu 10
Morgan Opinion Poll 90
Morgan, Hugh Matheson 6-8, 13, 109-114, 118
Moss, Irene 119
Mount Todd 103-104
Moynihan, Martin 60-63
Muirhead, James 42
Mulally, John 101
Mullenjarli People 100
Murray Islands 58
Murray, William 21
Murrayians 17
Mutitjulu People 40
Myall Creel Murders 20

N

Nabalco 28
Nairn, Bede 50
National Aboriginal Conference 40, 41, 81
National Aboriginal Consultative Committee 33
National Farmers Federation 86, 106, 125

143

National Civic Council 27
Native title 72, 82, 84, 125, 128
Nettheim, Garth 58
Newspoll 9, 90
Ngunnawal People 102
Nippon Mining and Metals 83
Noonkanbah 37-38
Normandy Poseidon 107
Northern Land Council 80, 83
Northern Territory 28, 40, 82-83, 95-97
Nullarbor Plain 94

O

Oceanic Negritos 17
O'Connor, Richard Edward 66
O'Donoghue, Lois 80, 83
Olympic Dam 93
O'Shane, Pat 80

P

Papua New Guinea 15, 17
Parngurr People 95
Passi, David 58, 59, 60
Passi, Sam 60
Pearson, Noel 81, 86
Perkins, Charles 6, 43, 119, 136
Perron, Marshall 83, 91, 117, 123
Pissants 76
Pitjantjatjara People 93
Pleistocene epoch 15
Prescott, john 11, 104
Press Gallery 53, 89
Privy Council 65
Punmu Comunity 95

Q

Queen (The) 44, 53, 68
Queensland 5, 60, 97-101
Queensland Coast Islands Declamatory Act 1985 60

R

Racial Discrimination Act 1975 34-35, 62, 72
Racism 3, 112, 118-119, 122, 136
Rae, Peter 92
Ralph, John 100
Ramsey, Alan 122-123
Referenda 25, 77, 94, 117
Reid, Alan 28, 29
Reid, Scott 105
Renison Goldfields 95
Returned Services League (RSL) 112
Reynolds, Henry 20, 135
Reynolds, Margaret 83, 125
Rice, James 60
Richardson, Graham 46
Riley, Rob 40, 81, 124
Ritchie, Manul 80
Rolph, Bruce 10
Roxby Downs 93
Royal Commission into Aboriginal Deaths in Custody 3, 12, 42-43
Rudall River 94
Russell, Don 124
Ryan, Lyndall 38, 40

S

Salee, Celvia 60
de la Salle College 49, 110
Salomon Brothers 10
Samuel Griffith Society 74, 136
Sansbury, Tauto 80

Santamaria, B.A. 27, 135
Saulwick Poll 9
Saunders, Sandra 81
Sharp, Nonie 58, 59, 60
Singleton, John 77, 78
South Australia 93
Stanner, William 31
Stephen, Alfred 28
Stevens, John 3
Stone, John 74
Stradbroke Island 5
Strapp, Terry 104
Strehlow, T.G.H. 18, 23
Sullivan, Alan 96
Sunday Herald Sun 9
Sydney Morning Herald 122
Sydney Opera House 5

T

Tasmania 92-93
Terra Nullius 28, 58, 71, 110
Tickner, Robert 4, 10, 43, 54, 78, 91, 96, 110, 114, 117, 126
Toohey, John Leslie 67, 71
Torres Strait Islands 31, 57, 59
Toyne, Phillip 78, 125
Tribunal (land) 126
Truganini 93
Turtle Farms Affair 31-33

U

Ularu National Park 40
United Nations 29, 34

V

Victoria 92
Viner, Ian 36

W

Wadi Wadi People 102
Waier Island 58

Walker, Frank 11, 78, 82, 127
Wallace, Alfred Russell 16
Walsh, Peter 8, 12, 72
Wangi People 8
Watson, John 80
Wattie Creek 2
Wentworth, W.C. 25
Weipa 97-99
West Australian Chamber of Mines and Energy 94
Western Australia 6, 37, 94-95
Western Mining Corporation 7, 93, 110
Whitlam, Edward Gough 1, 2, 12, 26, 27-36
Wik People 6, 97-99
Wilcannia 134
Wilkes, Ted 80
Willis, Ralph 78
Wills, Mike 10
Wilson, Ian 37
Wiradjuri People 101
Woodward, Edward 30, 34
World Congress of Indigenous People 38
World Council of Churches 38
World Heritage listing 36, 94, 107
Wybalenna 92

Y

Yirrkala People 28, 30, 58
Yorta Yorta People 92
Yunupingu, Galarrwuy 80, 130

Z

Zapopan NL 103-104